LETTERS *from the* HEAD *and* HEART

WRITINGS OF THOMAS JEFFERSON

LETTERS *from the* HEAD *and* HEART

WRITINGS OF THOMAS JEFFERSON

by Andrew Burstein

Preface by Peter S. Onuf

THOMAS JEFFERSON FOUNDATION

Monticello Monograph Series

2002

Library of Congress Cataloging-in-Publication Data

Burstein, Andrew.
    Letters from the head and heart: writings of Thomas Jefferson / by Andrew Burstein ;
preface by Peter S. Onuf.
      p. cm. -- (Monticello monograph series)
    Includes bibliographical references and index.
    ISBN 1-882886-20-8 (alk. paper)
      1. Jefferson, Thomas, 1743-1826--Personality. 2. Jefferson, Thomas, 1743-1826--
Literary art. I. Title. II. Series.

E332.2 .B86 2002
973.4'6'092--dc21

                                     2002034002

ON THE COVER

Inset portrait: *Thomas Jefferson* by Jean-Antoine Houdon, 1789 (Thomas Jefferson Foundation).
Background portraits: *Maria Cosway* by Francesco Bartolozzi, engraver, after Richard Cosway, 1785
(Thomas Jefferson Foundation) and *John Adams* by Alonzo Chappel after Gilbert Stuart and Bass
Otis, 1862 (Thomas Jefferson Foundation).

Designed by Gibson Design Associates.
Edited and coordinated by Beth L. Cheuk.

This book was made possible by support from the
Martin S. and Luella Davis Publications Endowment.

Distributed by
The University of North Carolina Press
Chapel Hill, North Carolina 27515-2288
1-800-848-6224

CONTENTS

PREFACE

*T*homas Jefferson is a famously elusive character. Modern biographers have described him as impenetrable and sphinx-like, a human bundle of paradoxes and contradictions. A master of self-control, Jefferson left us few obvious clues to his inner life: many account books, but no personal diary; an incomplete autobiography, drafted in 1821, that was designed to set the public record straight but was devoid of reflection on his private life; a vast archive of personal letters, but frustratingly few confessional moments or spontaneous, passionate outbursts.

Take Jefferson's famous "Head and Heart" letter to Maria Cosway, one of the great love letters in American literature. If ever there were a moment of self-revelation in the Jefferson canon, this would be it. And the effects are certainly dazzling. Yet even though the "heart" gets the best lines and is generally acclaimed the victor in its exchange with the "head," the literary artifice of the dialogue form is as mystifying to us as it must have been for Cosway. Where was the "real" Jefferson in this elaborate performance? Why didn't *he* just say what he meant? Of course, this is just what frustrated biographers would say as they read this letter—and everything else Jefferson wrote. There might be some good material here to serve scholars' other interpretative purposes (for instance, in Jefferson's discussion of the heart's role in the Revolution: "If our country, when pressed with wrongs at the point of the bayonet, had been governed by it's heads instead of it's hearts, where should we have been now?"). But we still don't know what *kind* of relationship he had with Cosway (were they actually lovers?), or why Jefferson's ardor cooled, or even what purpose the "Head and Heart" letter was supposed to serve.

Andrew Burstein is a different kind of biographer. His *Inner Jefferson: Portrait of a Grieving Optimist* succeeds where other biographies fail precisely because he seeks his subject *in* his writing, not *through* it. While psychologically self-absorbed modern readers define their "authentic," natural selves in opposition to the artificial, socially-sanctioned roles they perform in the so-called "real" world, Jefferson self-consciously fashioned himself according to the literary and cultural conventions of his day. A little healthy skepticism about modern solipsism—our love affair with our supposedly unique, authentic selves—goes a long way toward making Jefferson and his contemporaries more accessible and familiar. Jefferson understood the difference between "private" and "public," home and the world, but he thought that the same self operated in both domains. His vision, as Burstein suggests in his brilliant reading of Jefferson's first inaugural address, "combined his sentimental vision of friendship with his prescription for republicanism," deploying "vocabulary drawn from literary and philosophical worlds to merge the two." Jefferson's premises, we would say, are holistic, not only by transcending the traditional distinction of rulers and ruled in the monarchical, aristocratic societies of the old regime, but also by merging man and citizen, heart and head, in the new republican dispensation. The title of Burstein's book thus may be a bit misleading, suggesting that it will offer the juicy revelations that modern readers expect to find in biographical exposés, but instead teaching us that we are looking for the wrong thing—a "real" person we can identify with—in all the wrong places. He plays with these expectations in his introduction, inviting the "curious reader to pursue either the private or public Jefferson," but warning the reader (in a sly parenthesis) that he or she will encounter "both … for the politician and the president could not have arisen without first a concerted effort to bring forth a personal style."

Burstein's major insight is that literary form was for Jefferson indistinguishable from the substance of his most cherished beliefs. He was a "humanist" who believed that words mattered, that they could link like-minded souls across vast distances, constituting bonds of friendship in an expansive and inclusive "republic of letters," itself an image of mankind's better future. To modern readers, the sentiment and feeling that inform Jefferson's public and political rhetoric may seem misplaced (we reserve our "feelings" for our personal lives), somewhat fatuous and high-sounding, a pattern for the meaningless nonsense that so often characterizes public discourse today. Do friendship, fellow-feeling, the "pure 'affection'" of the first inaugural in fact make us a nation? Does the Jeffersonian gospel of reconciliation and love address the underlying causes of the diseases then afflicting the American body politic, wracked by the spasms and convulsions of party politics? Does all his talk about healing mean anything, or does it merely disguise Jefferson's own partisan purposes? Burstein is, appropriately, equivocal on this point. On one hand, "human physiology was integral to his political philosophy," and notions of sympathy and harmony derived from this way of thinking were crucial to Jefferson's conception of human sociability generally. Yet, on the other, Jefferson himself was "an angry partisan" who was convinced that his High Federalist enemies were determined to destroy the republic. We may all be "federalists" and "republicans"—according to Jefferson's harmonizing definitions of these terms—but High Federalists were beyond the pale and "he wanted them gone."

Letters from the Head and Heart is the best short biography we have of Jefferson. Its ostensibly modest goal, to introduce us to "eighteenth-century culture as it was lived and felt," opens up exciting new vistas to modern readers. The book's organization is also rather modest. Burstein has selected a sample of Jefferson writings, offering sensible commentaries on each text—"sensible" both in the sense of being reasonable and in uncovering a world of feeling and sentiment now lost to us. But notice the apparently promiscuous mix of private letters and public documents, and notice how Burstein's reading of one sort of text illuminates the other. The artful transitions from one commentary to the next reinforce our developing sense that the distinctions we make between private and public are profoundly misleading, that Jefferson himself is equally present in them all.

Has Burstein resolved all our questions about Jefferson? This could hardly be expected. The paradoxes and contradictions have not disappeared, however much better we may grasp their sources. The visionary Jefferson had more than a few blind spots—indeed, seeing things the way Jefferson saw them *depended* on not seeing discomfiting and disconfirming realities that were conspicuous to critical commentators then and now. And, yes, questions about his personal life will almost certainly remain unanswered. But we know much more now than we did before Andrew Burstein began his literary detective work. If we are ever to find a plausible approximation of the "real" or "inner" Jefferson, it will be by carefully listening to what he has told us, in his own words.

— Peter S. Onuf
University of Virginia

Jefferson's Cabinet at Monticello (Robert C. Lautman/Thomas Jefferson Foundation, Inc.)

INTRODUCTION

*P*erhaps no one's words are quite so prized in American history as those of Thomas Jefferson, and yet a modern reader necessarily understands them in a context that is not Jefferson's. To fully appreciate Jefferson's prose requires that the reader shed his or her twenty-first century skin and try to encounter eighteenth-century culture as it was lived and felt. This is a daunting task, but worthwhile.

Letters from the Head and Heart: Writings of Thomas Jefferson is such an undertaking. The literary and emotional world that Jefferson knew constitutes the soil, and Jefferson's writings, the flower, of this book. The nature metaphor is one that Jefferson himself might have chosen; when his eldest grandchild, Anne, gave birth in 1810, he wrote to her preciously of the fragility of life and the passage of time: "The flowers come forth like the belles of the day, have their short reign of beauty and splendor, and retire like them to the more interesting office of reproducing their like."[1]

Over the course of eight decades, Jefferson developed and amplified his philosophy of life through the careful and constant application of his pen. What assumptions he held, how he fashioned a literary persona, how he made himself understood—these questions form the essence of our investigation, and are intended to lead the curious reader to pursue either the private or public Jefferson (or both). For the politician and president could not have arisen without first a concerted effort to bring forth a personal style.

Jefferson wrote some eighteen thousand letters of which we are aware, and painstakingly maintained at Monticello a 656-page index of every letter written and received from 1783 until his death in 1826.[2] Letter writing represents the desire for intimacy as well as the need to act, to publicize one's thoughts, to leave some trace of one's life. Thus if we are going to try to understand Jefferson, it makes sense to start with his commitment to epistolary culture—to familiar letter writing. His vision of how the world was, and how it could be, is best gleaned from this rich body of writing.

To a well-bred American of the revolutionary generation, letter writing was an essential means of establishing a public reputation, displaying refinement, and demonstrating the proper balance between self-confidence and a desirable humility. When Jefferson wished to show his regard for John Adams's son-in-law, William S. Smith, he wrote to James Madison: "You can judge of Smith's abilities by his letters."[3] At a time when distance often prevented people from conducting affairs in person, letters were, in effect, conversation, an implied trust; they could convey factual information, or they could share confidences and reveal profound sentiment. Form—such as the ritualized salutation "Dear Sir"—suggests to us constraint, but that does not imply coldness in the body of the letter, just as the present-day closing, "Yours sincerely," is formulaic but used quite warmly in many personal letters. Indeed, then as now, subtlety mattered.

Jefferson mixed style and substance, and it is our challenge to locate the humanity and originality in his craft. Ultimately, to understand the full meaning of his richest letters requires that we separate the "postured" prose from other, more genuine communication. This posturing was the studied effort, in the mode of the day, to appear to reveal a candid, leisurely "self." This style of writing exists side-by-side in Jefferson's letters with the more demonstrative act of "reaching out" to another being. Another way to describe this difference is to contrast neoclassical friendship and the spirit of romantic individuality: the former communicates eloquently, while hesitating, deliberating, and emulating conversational prose; the latter is spontaneous and artless, and far more rare among Jefferson's generation.

This is not to say that Jefferson is impenetrable. His use of metaphors and often-repeated phrases, and his clear commitment to the art of self-expression, reveal that he finds a certain delight in stirring—not just impressing—the recipients of his letters. Above all, his interest in moral philosophy and his humanism (the political idea that the quality of life and the dignity of all people matter), should convince us that Thomas Jefferson did not put words to paper without intending them to be believed; over and over he uses such words as *pure, honest, sincere,* and *free*. He celebrated knowledge. He embraced the global quest for improvement.

Jefferson read and wrote about the sources of inspiration that animated such great minds as Homer, Sir Isaac Newton, and Benjamin Franklin. His feeling for beauty in nature was more than scientific, and he understood the musicality of words as a means to charm or awaken the emotions. As a public man and political partisan, Jefferson knew the danger of words when unleashed, and yet many times over the course of his long life the misuse of his correspondence caused embarrassments (the loss of George Washington's friendship, for one).

Perhaps proof that Jefferson accepted the risk of self-exposure is a line he wrote in 1816 to the Quaker George Logan, who had inadvertently betrayed a confidence contained in an earlier letter. "We are careless, incorrect, in haste, perhaps under some transient excitement, and we hazard things without reflection," Jefferson wrote his repentant friend, adding that these errors are "without consequence in the bosom of a friend."⁴ It was a most noble rationale to ease his friend's mind, and worthy of Jefferson at his best.

Jefferson was a man of strong convictions and rarely careless in any activity, in spite of the impression he wished to convey to Logan. His powerful prose is the immortal part of him and the best artifact we own. It affords us, even now, the prospect of understanding this curious and intriguing eighteenth-century man.

— ANDREW BURSTEIN

Declaration of Independence, *John Binns, publisher, and James Barton Longacre, engraver, 1819 (Thomas Jefferson Foundation, Inc.)*

Chapter One

DECLARATION OF INDEPENDENCE

When in the course of human events, it becomes necessary for one people to dissolve the political bands which have connected them with another, and to assume among the powers of the earth the separate and equal station to which the laws of nature and of nature's God entitle them, a decent respect to the opinions of mankind requires that they should declare the causes which impel them to the separation.

When the thirty-three-year-old Thomas Jefferson composed his most famous public document in 1776, he did not aim to invent a nation on his own terms, but rather to adapt common sentiments and specific judgments that reflected the consensus of the Second Continental Congress, then meeting in Philadelphia. Though his theme was unoriginal, the Virginian's vibrant vocabulary arose from his appreciation of human nature as much as it profited from his superior legal training; his literary gift further ensured the rhythm and balance that made his composition memorable.[5]

The Declaration of Independence was meant as a lawful rationale for political disunion. It opens with a rather straightforward statement concerning "the laws of nature and of nature's God"—the source of Jefferson's political faith. It asserts the essential equality of nations while invoking "respect to the opinions of mankind"—those who comprised the draftsman's larger audience. Predominantly concerned with *individual* rights and *individual* impulses, Jefferson perceived "the course of human events" as a history that was felt, that was experienced, that was profoundly human. That was why governments, in his view, were "instituted among men, deriving their just powers from the consent of the governed." It was not a select few who were endowed with rights, but "all men"—or, in the more modern sense, all citizens. These citizens, then, had arrived at a crucial point in their history where their integrity as human beings was gravely threatened. They had "causes which impel them" to a dramatic "separation," matters of the utmost urgency.

The ensuing great American catechism pronounces that all human beings possess "certain inalienable rights." (Jefferson had first written "inherent and inalienable rights," and his Congressional editors altered his phrase slightly.) Jefferson proceeded to characterize the most fundamental of human rights (and here Congress moved not a letter) as "life, liberty, and the pursuit of happiness."

While the phrase has been immortalized, its meaning is self-evident solely on the surface. Only in context can we comprehend just what "pursuit of happiness" meant to Jefferson and the revolutionary generation. It should be noted that later in the same paragraph Jefferson repeats the word *happiness*, coupling it this time with *safety*; government provides "safety and happiness" to its citizens en masse. *Happiness*, then, was a concept that could be easily generalized. In American newspapers during the decades leading to the Revolution, *happiness* was often identified as an elusive treasure in every human life, a quality that could never be counted on, that was fleeting at best. So for Jefferson to employ the word *happiness* as part of an "inalienable right" was to make it more than a political virtue—it was a moral imperative.

In his widely read *Essay Concerning the Human Understanding*, published near the end of the previous century, English philosopher John Locke had titled two different subsections of his work "A constant Determination to a Pursuit of Happiness, no Abridgement of Liberty" and "The Necessity of pursuing true Happiness, the Foundation of Liberty." Thus, there was ample precedent for associating happiness with an idealized political community.

The Anglican clergyman and author Laurence Sterne (1713–1768) specialized in crafting literary scenes in which acts of sublime charity took place. He expressed sympathetic communion between elite men and the more ordinary members of society. Jefferson owned Sterne's *Sermons* from 1765, and the clergyman's popular novels *Tristram Shandy* and *A Sentimental Journey* were Jefferson's great favorites. Sterne, curiously, opened his first published sermon with the refrain, "The great pursuit of man is after happiness; it is the first and strongest desire of his nature;—in every stage of his life, he searches for it, as for hid treasure." Jefferson did not coin the phrase "pursuit of happiness," nor did he claim originality in his Declaration. We can acknowledge, however, that the affecting language he chose drew upon an idiom that was in vogue, and that Jefferson enlarged upon its previous meanings.

Jefferson's "happiness" connoted security. He did not separate happiness, whether individual or social, from reasoned calculation and calm introspection. The head and heart operated in tandem. Good rules flowed from the active mind; to pursue happiness was to commit consciously to the exercise of a generous, outward-directed spirit. Thus self-examination preceded public realization of happiness. Jefferson was, in this sense, both Lockean and Sternean.

From its unforgettable opening, the Declaration proceeds to contrast American patience with British inflexibility and impulsiveness. This is where Jefferson's emotionalism is a euphonic, rhythmic piece of profound propaganda. At the feet of King George III, symbolically blamed for all oppression carried out by his ministers, Jefferson lays the list of grievances felt by the people of an invaded land. As he writes, he is keenly conscious that the Battles of Lexington and Concord had taken place more than a year earlier, and British troops were poised to invade and occupy New York.

To a "candid world," by which he means an open-minded world, Jefferson shoots verbs, one upon the next: the tyrant king "has refused," "has forbidden," "has dissolved," "has endeavored to prevent," "has obstructed," "has combined with others to subject us," "has plundered our seas, ravaged our coasts, burnt our towns, and destroyed the lives of our people." The sense of outrage at the combined "injuries and usurpations" is heightened as the text moves forward, and the threat to the land is made more apparent: the suffering Americans lay "exposed to all the dangers of invasion from without and convulsions within." The world's most powerful navy had supplied the first threat, and the active loyalist forces at home added the "convulsions."

Again, it is worth pausing to consider Jefferson's choice of words and to explore their temporal context. The people of 1776 knew a kind of vulnerability that twenty-first-century Americans can scarcely appreciate. Because medical knowledge was quite limited, they endured disease and the deaths of loved ones on an immense scale. The word *convulsions* suggested a host of visceral sensations to those who read the Declaration and those who heard it read in public. At the time, the nervous system was seen as mysterious and invisibly powerful, the not-quite-tangible link between the brain and the soul. Thus, health and hope required overcoming natural shocks and regaining control through exertion of the body's defenses. If America was perceptibly vulnerable and deeply troubled by loyalist enemies in its midst, then "convulsions" represented spiritual disharmony as well as physical decay and dissolution.

In addition to the king's responsibility for "convulsions" within the American body politic, he was also responsible for having "sent hither swarms of new officers to harass our people and eat out their substance." Once more, the language Jefferson used to describe an enemy's barbarity or bestiality suggests a medical emergency for which eighteenth-century medicine was insufficient. Overpowering "swarms" were sent "to harass" (meaning "to exhaust") the people and, like a cancer, to "eat out their substance." Though the king himself may not have caused such conditions, Jefferson's rhetorical counterattack was intended to implicate him, so as to personalize an evil. His Declaration was designed to be militant in order to inspire youths across the former British colonies to enlist in the new, undermanned Continental Army.

The extravagance in Jefferson's language is apparent, too, in his depiction of British-allied Native American Indians as "savages, whose known rule of warfare is an undistinguished destruction of all ages, sexes, and conditions." By pointing to the need to protect women and children from those who would kill without conscience, Jefferson aroused a chivalrous response. Just a few years earlier, a famous son of liberty, Dr. Joseph Warren, had appealed on similar grounds in an oration delivered before a crowd of resolute Bostonians to commemorate the "massacre" of five protesters by British soldiers. Warren outlined a verbal picture of societal ruin as apocalyptic as Jefferson's references to harassing swarms and Indians on the warpath: "Language is too feeble to paint the emotions of our souls," Warren wailed, "when our streets were stained with the blood of our brethren,—when our ears were wounded by the groans of the dying, and our eyes were tormented with the sight of the mangled bodies of the dead.—When our alarmed imaginations presented to our view our houses wrapped in flames,—our children subjected to the barbarous caprice of the raging soldiery."[6] Living without liberty was, to Warren as to Jefferson, the moral equivalent to death. Being subject to imagined Indian depredations was, in the Declaration, an even more horrid fate than to be impaled by British steel.

Insofar as the Declaration was wartime propaganda, the polemicist from Virginia declined to debate whether the Indians were justifiably disaffected from colonial Americans. Indeed, this time his Congressional editors went beyond even the histrionic Jefferson, in prefacing his short paragraph on Indian methods with the phrase, "He [the king] has excited domestic insurrection among us." As Jefferson had already raised the specter of "convulsions within," Congress deepened the image by assigning to hostile Indians the penchant for "insurrection" when tempted by the British invader.

Immediately following this harangue, Jefferson proposed to blame the king for African-American slavery as well. Congress, however, expunged this long paragraph because of significant opposition among legislators from the Deep South. The king, wrote Jefferson, "has waged cruel war against human nature itself, violating its most sacred rights of life and liberty in the persons of a distant people who never offended him, captivating and carrying them into slavery in another hemisphere, or to incur miserable death in their transportation hither." Again, choosing language to strike at the heart (favoring emotional impact over literal truth), he minimized Americans' active role in the slave trade and enlarged on the king's passive complicity.

At this juncture, Jefferson reaches a crescendo in the composition. America had appealed, he wrote, to the "native justice and magnanimity" of its former British brethren. He tells the "candid world" that it was America that was abandoned by Britain, not the other way around. In the most affecting sense—as always, Jefferson's greatest power was reserved for moral persuasion—it was the British authorities who had turned away, turning their backs on the utterly decent colonists. Britain, though powerful, had proven "deaf to the voice of justice and consanguinity"—senses dulled and the blood ties of generations ignored and forgotten. As Dr. Warren stated in his Boston Massacre oration, the enemy could only exhibit "barbarous caprice" after having lost all fraternal feeling or remembrance of blood ties.

Beyond this, Jefferson asserted with unprecedented lyricism: "These facts have given the last stab to agonizing affection"—he was re-emphasizing the colonists' hurt and vulnerability—"and manly spirit bids us to renounce forever these unfeeling brethren." What distinguished Americans was their feeling nature; they were self-protectively responding to unwarranted persecution from those who did not feel or could not empathize. For unknown reasons, Congress deleted from the final text Jefferson's lively allusion to the agony of betrayal.

How, then, to conclude this proud, righteous, passionately unyielding document? The new "representatives of the United States of America"—this was the first time that the nation had named itself—acknowledged that they and their fellow citizens constituted "free and independent states," with all the rights and power of any other sovereign political entity. And to seal their joint resolve, Jefferson provided a final sanctifying refrain, in which "we mutually pledge to each other our lives, our fortunes, and our sacred honor."

While the soft-spoken legislator would not be widely known as the author of the Declaration of Independence until his election to the presidency in 1801, Jefferson's masterful way with words had already won approbation from other, equally ardent delegates to the Continental Congress. In the fall of that dramatic year of 1776, he returned to his native state, where he applied his skills, and his pen, to the revision of Virginia's laws. Amid a war that would eventually find its way literally to his doorstep, he also endeavored, with only marginal success, to cultivate crops and a sense of private harmony on his lofty mountain plantation.

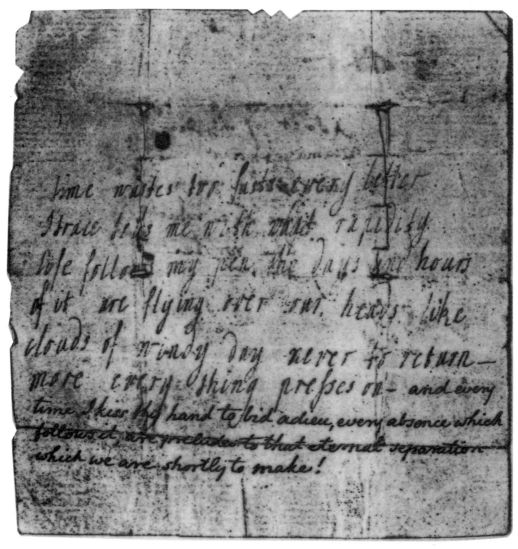

Letter written by Thomas and Martha Jefferson sometime before her death on
September 6, 1782 (courtesy of the James Monroe Museum and Memorial Library.)

Chapter Two

"LIFE FOLLOWS MY PEN"

Time wastes too fast: every letter
I trace tells me with what rapidity
life follows my pen. The days and hours
of it are flying over our heads like
clouds of a windy day never to return—
more. Every thing presses on—and every
time I kiss thy hand to bid adieu, every absence which
follows it, are preludes to that eternal separation
which we are shortly to make![7]

This is Jeffersonian sentiment, but it was borrowed from novelist Laurence Sterne's rambling tale of wit and conscience, *Tristram Shandy*. First copied by Jefferson into his Commonplace Book (a personalized scrapbook of collected sayings) in the early 1780s, these moving lines were rendered into a succinct dialogue by a dying Martha (Patty) Jefferson and her tormented husband as they copied them together. To appreciate what Sterne's words of tenderness meant to Thomas Jefferson is to penetrate the late eighteenth century's veneer of stoic dignity.[8]

Sterne and Jefferson emphasized self-knowledge in their writings. Both saw the world as a place of inconstancy and turmoil, rescued by human compassion and sympathetic communion. In a 1787 letter to nephew Peter Carr, Jefferson asserted: "the writings of Sterne particularly form the best course of morality that ever was written."[9] Perhaps the importance of Sterne to Jefferson is shown in a brief vignette. While in France, in the mid-1780s, Jefferson acted out a poignant scene from Sterne's *A Sentimental Journey*, giving alms to a Franciscan monk in

Calais, just where Sterne's literary alter-ego, the "Sentimental traveller" Yorick, had done the same.

Sterne was contagious. His comic gift exposed all kinds of human follies, piling picaresque descriptions of characters one upon the other. Dr. Slop was "a little, squat, uncourtly figure … with a breadth of back and a sesquipedality of belly." Sterne taunted and toyed with his readers, taking five chapters, for instance, to transport his characters down a staircase. It was all done to relieve the tension of a life that was fleeting; the author himself suffered from a deadly, debilitating tuberculosis and wrote self-consciously to prolong his own life. Only death could not be treated with a light heart: "Philosophy has a fine saying for everything," the character Tristram narrates. "For Death, it has an entire set."

"Time wastes too fast" is the one vignette from Sterne that Jefferson elected to include in a Commonplace Book devoted primarily to traditional wisdom (much of it in Greek and Latin). In copying it, the Virginian was clearly affected by Sterne's melancholy drama, twice using exclamation marks in place of the author's colon.

Why is the vignette from Sterne so important? Most of his contemporaries regarded Jefferson as soft-spoken and mild-tempered, but resilient and imperturbable, even impassive. Almost no one commented on his rather unstoical, nostalgic streak. This sentimental side is shown in his remembrance of his elder sister, Jane. Though she died when he was twenty-two, as a grandfather he still spoke of her to family, remarking that "some sacred air" in church recalled her "sweet voice" to him.

He married the widow Martha Wayles Skelton in 1772, and they enjoyed what he called much later "ten years of unchequered happiness." But Martha was a petite woman with a fragile constitution. In the summer of 1782, after her sixth pregnancy, she remained bedridden, slowly losing strength. There is also speculation that she may have languished from tuberculosis. On September 6, Thomas Jefferson wrote with precision in his Account Book, "My dear wife died this day at 11H—45' A.M."[10]

Sometime prior to her death, the two Jeffersons took turns writing out the passage from Sterne. Martha wrote the first part, "Time wastes too fast," exchanging the pen after "every thing presses on." In his meticulous handwriting, her husband picked up with the words "and every time I kiss thy hand to bid adieu," exclaiming at the bottom that he had surrendered to fate and awaited their final parting.

This is one of few existing records of Martha Jefferson's handwriting. Her despairing husband apparently destroyed what remained of their intimate correspondence, perhaps in the fashion of the day to assist the grieving process. However, he retained this one souvenir of their love, a four-and-one-half-inch square piece of paper, and enclosed in it a lock of her hair and a lock of hair belonging to one of their children who had died in infancy.[11]

Jefferson kept Martha's deathbed adieu in a compartment inside a private cabinet in his bedroom. One can imagine him folding and unfolding it, holding and examining it, countless times over the next forty-four years. Jefferson's one surviving daughter, her mother's namesake, found the paper upon Jefferson's death in 1826.

Maria Cosway *by L. Schiavonotti, engraver after Richard Cosway, c.1794 (Thomas Jefferson Foundation, Inc.)*

Chapter Three

"My Head and My Heart"

Heart. And what more sublime delight than to mingle tears with one whom the hand of heaven hath smitten! To watch over the bed of sickness & to beguile it's tedious & it's painful moments! To share our bread with one to whom misfortune left none! This world abounds indeed with misery: to lighten it's burthen we must divide it with one another.[12]

A Dutch acquaintance in 1784 described the widower Jefferson as a man who had "retired from fashionable society ..., his sole diversion being that offered by belles lettres."[13] In the summer of that year, however, urged by friends, Jefferson accepted a diplomatic appointment and sailed for France with his daughter Martha (Patsy) and servant James Hemings. At first, his bookish French and a disheartening winter (he called it "torpid," in a letter to James Monroe) kept Jefferson from enjoying Paris. After a time, though, Benjamin Franklin's successor as American minister to the court of King Louis XVI furnished an impressive townhouse and plunged into the European salon culture, meeting men and women of manners and intellect, and eagerly participating in their literary-philosophic discussions.

One of the talented women he met was Maria Louisa Catherine Cecilia Hadfield Cosway, an Italian-born English painter, twenty-seven years old, sixteen years his junior. She was in a loveless marriage and was apparently as taken with the learned Virginian as he was with her. She was slim and graceful, and spoke a musical mélange of European dialects. The two went on walks and picnics, attended theater and museums. On one intimate outing, Jefferson apparently tried to vault a fence and fell, breaking his wrist. The circumstances are hazy, but to a male acquaintance Jefferson hinted, "How the right hand became disabled would be a long story for the left to tell. It was by one of those follies from which good cannot come, but ill may."[14]

Not long after, Jefferson was surprised to learn that the Cosways were to return to London. Emotionally conflicted, the right-handed Jefferson wrote, with his left hand, a twelve-page letter set in the form of a dialogue. This stylish, evocative composition, dated October 12, 1786, is both a testament to sentimental friendship and a window to the inner life of the man who fashioned it.[15] "My dear Madam," it begins, lamenting his having just performed the "sad office" of handing her into her carriage. A forlorn Jefferson attests to feeling "more dead than alive" at their parting. At the end of the first paragraph, he announces that he is seated at his fireside where a dialogue has been taking place between "my Head and my Heart."

The head speaks of the dangers of committing to a friendship and of the imprudence of engaging in any activity bound to bring pain. No matter what the merit or refreshing honesty possessed by the object of one's affections, "you rack our whole system when you are parted from those you love."

The heart, of course, objects to the head's excess of "prudence." How could one calculate the value of such a reverie as that which had been occasioned by the beautiful scenery they shared on the warm day when Jefferson and Mrs. Cosway had ridden together beyond the city? "Every moment was filled with something agreeable. The wheels of time moved on with a rapidity of which those of our carriage gave but a faint idea, and yet in the evening, when one took a retrospect of the day, what a mass of happiness had we travelled over!" The movement of time oriented Jefferson emotionally; in this case it consoled, it healed, it brought on "a mass of happiness."

Calculating or quantifying "happiness" was a vague and uncertain operation. Indeed, the pursuit of happiness, a moral condition in Jefferson's Declaration, was less secure here. He goes on to say that she had been "chiding" him amid all this "happiness." Happiness, in Jefferson's vocabulary, has too many general uses and so is reduced in energy and authority by its variety. To describe happiness in the most personally satisfying way, Jefferson preferred another word: delight.

In the longest unimpeded passage in the letter, the heart works up the nerve to declare that there is no more sublimely satisfying act in a human life than to partake in an expression of true generosity, especially toward someone who is suffering, who can be spiritually rescued by the unselfish commitment of one heart to another. This is vintage Jeffersonian (and Sternean) sentiment: "And what more sublime delight than to mingle tears with one whom the hand of heaven hath smitten!"

It is "delight" rather than "happiness" that Jefferson chooses to express the height of moral feeling. Elsewhere, he uses "delight" to convey his desire to live out his life as a student of nature: "Nature intended for me the tranquil pursuits of science, by rendering them my supreme delight." Similarly, the poetic joy of reading Homer in the original Greek was "this rich source of my delight."

The heart's plaint continues: "To watch over the bed of sickness, & to beguile it's tedious & it's painful moments! To share our bread with one to whom misfortune left none! This world abounds indeed with misery: to lighten it's burthen we must divide it with one another." Again, it is an unselfish bestowal of the self that produces the inward feeling of real satisfaction.

The head cautions: "This is not a world to live in random as you do." But the heart can only find relief through "the solace of our friends!" It is a dynamic and enduring sensation to be thus "penetrated with their assiduities and attentions!" Exclamatory statements accompany Jefferson's references to the joy of grief, in seeming disavowal of the stupor into which he was thrown when his wife died four years earlier: "When Heaven has taken from us some object of our love," he writes Mrs. Cosway, "how sweet it is to have a bosom whereon to recline our heads, and into which we may pour the torrent of our tears! Grief, with such a comfort, is almost a luxury!" The value of friendship, in other words, made up for the pain of loss.

The head contended that life was smooth only when one insulated himself from others: "Friendship is but another name for an alliance with the follies and misfortunes of others." But the heart refuses to "think," to operate with such repellent supervision and caution: "nobody will care for him who cares for nobody," it answers. The letter reaches a new loftiness once Jefferson asserts with momentous optimism that "friendship is precious not only in the shade but in the sunshine of life: and thanks to a benevolent arrangement of things, the greater part of life is sunshine."

The heart draws one more comparison between the unfeeling head and its own sense of compassionate commitment. Here is another good example of Jefferson's ability in crafting images: "Let the gloomy Monk, sequestered from the world, seek unsocial pleasures in the bottom of his cell! Let the sublimated philosopher grasp visionary happiness while pursuing phantoms dressed in the garb of truth! Their supreme wisdom is supreme folly: and they mistake for happiness the mere absence of pain." Once again, Jefferson wrestles with the meaning of "happiness" and notes that it is a philosophic abstraction—what sometimes passes for happiness is the mere absence of heartache, something less than happiness. In this way, he believed, so-called great minds were too easily satisfied with surface pleasures; real happiness must be profoundly felt. Had the head even once felt "the solid pleasure of one generous spasm of the heart," it would know the inferior value of all its "frigid speculations."

The head is satisfied doing its "miserable arithmetic" to derive a happiness that can exist without friendship. The heart, on the contrary, is closer to the cause of nature—always Jefferson's standard for perfect order in the moral universe. He writes: "When nature assigned us [head and heart] the same habitation [the physical body], she gave us over it a divided empire. To you she allotted the field of science, to me that of morals …. Morals were too essential to the happiness of man to be risked on the uncertain combinations of the head." Certainty belonged only to natural morals, with which the heart was allied.

"My Head and My Heart" is Jefferson at his most charming, but he also adopts in the letter a moralistic tone that is interesting to compare with the language of the Declaration. In both instances, Jefferson highlights human vulnerability, either invoking a sense of justice (in the Declaration) or the correctness of benevolent agitation (in the dialogue) to solve a moral dilemma. His writings suggest a conviction that one must take chances in order for moral progress to result; the alternative is tame submission to power and authority. Indeed, he writes to Maria Cosway that the American Revolution could not have been won without the investment of the heart. The head had coldly calculated Britain's "wealth and numbers," while the fearless heart had supplied "enthusiasm" to counter that factual advantage; in doing so, writes Jefferson, "We saved our country."

Mrs. Cosway's response to the masterful letter was appreciative but subdued and wholly unremarkable. Jefferson wrote shorter, but equally suggestive letters over the next few months, leaving off his signature when he feared interception at the notoriously insecure post office (he had confided "My Head and My Heart" to a London-bound friend whose discretion he could trust). In a letter of November 19, 1786, he announced that she was receiving the "first homage" of his right hand, still in pain but functional. On November 29, he enchanted her, saying "I am never happier than when I commit myself into dialogue with you, tho' but in imagination." The familiar letter was, of course, a substitute for direct verbal conversation. To tell someone in a letter that one was imagining the other's presence was entirely conventional, but no less endearing. He urged her, too, to write to him "without reserve." And on December 24, he fantasized: "If I cannot be with you in reality, I will in imagination."[16]

The months passed, and Jefferson's passion seems to have cooled somewhat. He saw the Anglo-Italian artist again during the final months of 1787 when she returned for an exhibition at the Louvre in Paris, but they did not spend much time together. After her return to London, they continued to write, though with fewer intimate references and greater formality.

However, Jefferson, ever the reliable correspondent, did not lose touch with this woman who had once captured his attention. He wrote his last letter to Maria Cosway in 1820, at the age of seventy-seven, once more speaking touchingly of friendship—this time with emphasis on his own mortal prospects: "For after one's friends are all gone before them, and our faculties leaving us too, one by one, why wish to linger in mere vegetation, as a solitary trunk in a desolate field, from which all it's former companions have disappeared." He signed off this letter with "the last and warmest wishes of an unchangeable friend."[17]

Over several decades, the subject of their correspondence had varied little. In the pure compilation of words, at least, the heart outperformed the head.

Martha Jefferson Randolph *by Thomas Sully, c.1836 (Thomas Jefferson Foundation, Inc.)*

Chapter Four

"My Dear Daughter"

I have nothing interesting to tell you from hence but that we are well, and how much we love you. From Monticello you have every thing to write about which I have any care. How do my young chestnut trees? How comes on your garden? How fare the fruit blossoms &c. I sent to Mr. Randolph, I think, some seed of the Bent-grass which is much extolled.[18]

In "My Head and My Heart," Jefferson gave a heartfelt recital of what his private mountain meant to him, though by that time he had not seen it for the better part of three years:

And our own dear Monticello, where has nature spread so rich a mantle under the eye? mountains, forests, rocks, rivers. With what majesty do we there ride above the storms! How sublime to look down into the workhouse of nature, to see her clouds, hail, snow, rain, thunder, all fabricated at our feet! And the glorious Sun, when rising as if out of a distant water, just gilding the tops of the mountains, and giving life to all nature!

The pleasures of the imagination were nowhere more satisfied than in the aesthetic challenge he took on when he built a stately sanctuary high above Shadwell and the Three-Notched Road, where he was born.

During the decade of the 1790s, Jefferson took the time to reconceive his well-ordered dream world, to bring system to nature. At this time, he added the distinctive dome to Monticello after a building he had seen in France, while doubling the size of the house. Still, he spent a good part of the years 1790–93 in New York and Philadelphia serving as President George Washington's secretary of state. With his younger daughter Maria (age twelve in 1790) often beside him, he urged his recently married daughter Martha (age eighteen) to keep an eye on Monticello.

The letters to Martha are tender, though some reveal his agitation over the polemical debates between Alexander Hamilton and himself. Their disputes tore apart the Washington administration, with Hamilton favoring a strong national government, and Jefferson, a mild administration that left citizens largely to their own devices. For Hamilton, power was meant to be consolidated; for Jefferson, it was meant to be diffused. During this trying period, Jefferson expressed to his elder daughter his strong desire to retire from public life, though he hung on as long as his emotional constitution allowed, explaining to her that "my retiring just when I had been attacked in the public [news]papers, would injure me in the eyes of the public, who would suppose … I had not tone of mind sufficient to meet slander."[19]

He invariably contrasts the clamor in Philadelphia with the promise of a quiet, unobtrusive life at Monticello, vowing, "when I see you, it will be never to part again." While Jefferson ultimately proved unable to resist public life, his letters to Martha Jefferson Randolph demonstrate how the beauty of the seasons at Monticello produced in his mind the image of family harmony and affinity—one of many Jeffersonian definitions of happiness.

"I am happy to find you are on good terms with your neighbors," he wrote the newly wedded Martha in the spring of 1791. "It is almost the most important circumstance in life, since nothing is so corroding as frequently to meet persons with whom one has any difference. The ill-will of a single neighbor is an immense drawback on the happiness of life, and therefore their good will cannot be bought too dear."[20] An ongoing concern with "the happiness of life" might seem to be conventional wisdom, but in Thomas Jefferson's case it was a governing concept of private as well as public affairs, and so we can imagine that his pronouncements on the subject possessed a deeper meaning.

In writing Martha, Jefferson associates happiness most often with domestic surroundings and kindly neighbors—it seemed that wherever he went, Jefferson sought inner peace by employing his literary imagination to recover his attachment to central Virginia. He often wrote critically of the unhealthy effects of urban conditions on the progress of human morals. To preserve rural simplicity was to preserve happiness; when combined with constant reading, immersion in the invigorating atmosphere of Monticello represented the ideal life to him. "However great my confidence is in the healthy air of Monticello," he wrote his daughter after a lapse of communication in the summer of 1791, "I am always happy to have my hopes confirmed by letter."[21]

Each of his letters began, "My dear daughter," or "Th:J to his dear Martha," or, in the case of one of January 1799, lacking a formal salutation but opening thus: "The object of this letter, my very dear Martha, is merely to inform you I am well and to convey to you the expressions of my love." Yet that was not his only motive. As politics heated up, Jefferson thought of his family letters as a respite from public strife.

Philadelphia had come to represent the opposite of rural retirement, and Monticello the antidote for partisan bitterness. Hearing from home was essential, he claimed, and lacking regular reports from his daughter "deprives me of the gleams of pleasure wanting to relieve the dreariness of this scene, where not a single occurrence is calculated to produce pleasing sensations." Philadelphia was particularly depressing for Jefferson during his vice presidency (1797–1801), when he felt the most powerless. In a May 1798 letter, he impatiently described the national capital as a place containing "every thing which can be disgusting;" by contrast, he recalled Monticello "and my dear family, comprising every thing which is pleasurable to me in this world."[22]

To Martha, he grew accustomed to writing of plantation business and the logistics of daily life. He trusted his elder daughter, along with her husband Thomas Mann Randolph, to manage his affairs. He credited her with sound judgment and placed responsibilities on her that ordinarily fell to sons in Jefferson's Virginia. Furthermore, he exposed her to the nastiness of national debate. With Maria, his younger daughter, he rarely discussed politics, preferring to encourage her to develop domestic skills. She was physically less strong than Martha, and this may have influenced Jefferson's treatment of her. A family friend, Margaret Bayard Smith, who was the same age as Maria, described her as "beautiful, simplicity and timidity personified when in company, but when alone with you of communicative and winning manners." Here is a typical example of the content of Jefferson's letters to Maria: "To you I rather indulge the effusions of the heart which tenderly loves you, which builds it's happiness on your's, and feels in every other object but little interest."

An obligatory contrast between Philadelphia and central Virginia follows, joined to his wishes that she locate life's meaning in a domesticated love (she had recently married her cousin Jack Eppes):

> *Without an object here which is not alien to me, and barren of every delight, I turn to your situation with pleasure in the midst of a good family which loves you, and merits all your love. Go on, my dear, in cultivating the invaluable possession of their affections. The circle of our nearest connections is the only one in which faithful and lasting affection can be found, one which will adhere to us under all changes and chances. It is therefore the only soil on which it is worth while to bestow much culture.*[23]

The nature metaphor with which Jefferson completes his thought demonstrates how important it was for him to associate the constructive purposes of the world he imagines with the nurturing of affections. He wants—desperately, it sometimes seems—for conversation within the political realm to rise to the level of optimistic sentiment that he readily attaches to domestic possibilities. But in the late 1790s, when his resentment toward the conflicts in public life was most constant, Jefferson could not restrain himself from burdening even Maria with these same thoughts:

> *Environed here [Philadelphia] in scenes of constant torment, malice and obloquy, worn down in a station where no effort to render service can aver any thing, I feel not that existence is a blessing but when something recalls my mind to my family or farm. This was the effect of your letter, and it's affectionate expressions kindled up all those feelings of love for you and our dear connections which now constitute the only real happiness of my life.*[24]

Despite his protestations to the contrary, Vice President Jefferson recognized that if his vision for a more harmonious human community were to be tried, he would have to remain in politics and contest his old friend John Adams for the presidency. Jefferson was less vexed by Adams the individual, however, than by the Federalist Party, the party of George Washington (still led philosophically by Alexander Hamilton). He believed the Federalists to be monarchical in tendencies, pro-British in spirit, and politically effete. On the contrary, he thought his own Democratic-Republican program was more representative of the simpler, homespun republican principles that animated the Americans of 1776.

Elbridge Gerry *by James Bogle, 1861, after John Vanderlyn (courtesy of Independence National Historical Park.)*

Chapter Five

REMOVING THE DEFAMATION FROM POLITICS

I shall make to you a profession of my political faith; in confidence that you will consider every future imputation on me of a contrary complexion, as bearing on its front the mark of falsehood & calumny.[25]

As the election of 1800 approached and the war of words continued to heat up in newspapers and widely printed pamphlets, candidate Jefferson sought to explain himself to a man he respected. Yet that man was one whom his opponent, President Adams, had assigned to a diplomatic mission on behalf of the administration: Elbridge Gerry of Massachusetts. Gerry was a signer of the Declaration of Independence and a delegate to the Constitutional Convention in 1787, although he had refused to sign in the second instance because he feared that the federal Constitution made the chief executive too strong. In the 1790s, he became a moderate Federalist, one of those Jefferson referred to as a "candid," or open-minded, Federalist.

In 1797, Adams sent Gerry to France on a diplomatic mission along with doctrinaire Federalists Charles Cotesworth Pinckney and John Marshall. Of the three, Gerry alone persevered in negotiations with the French revolutionaries in what became known as the XYZ affair. Pinckney and Marshall felt insulted by the French and sailed home, while Gerry stayed on, endeavoring to prevent Franco-American war.

Jefferson sympathized with the French Revolution in spite of its excesses, and he appreciated Gerry's decent intentions. Following Gerry's return, Jefferson wrote him in January 1799, attempting to extend their areas of agreement by suggesting that he was a man with whom Gerry could reason. Jefferson also claimed that the Federalist press, especially in New England, had grossly misrepresented his own politics. It was a letter at once mild and forceful.

"Our very long intimacy," Jefferson appealed, "as fellow-laborers in the same cause, the recent expressions of mutual confidence which had preceded your mission, the interesting course which that had taken, & particularly & personally as it regarded yourself, made me anxious to hear from you on your return." He came immediately to his point: he did not want Gerry to believe Federalist rumors, for Jefferson had "during the whole of your absence, as well as since your return, been a constant butt for every shaft of calumny which malice & falsehood could form, & the presses, public speakers, or private letters disseminate."

The nature of American politics at this moment was unusually discourteous. Pseudonymous columnists were quite abusive with language. Pro-Jefferson writers branded Adams a "mock Monarch" and "hoary-headed incendiary," while those for Adams labeled Jefferson a "false philosopher" and "infidel." Federalist Noah Webster wrote that if Jefferson were elected, he would bring "a greater scourge to society than a pestilence." In the midst of this heated dialogue, in the summer of 1798, the Federalist-dominated Congress passed the Alien and Sedition Laws: the first was designed to combat French revolutionary influence in America, by imprisoning or expelling any foreigner suspected of political agitation; the latter made it a criminal offense to criticize the Adams administration, either verbally or on paper.

Sensitive to the emotional impact of words, Jefferson eagerly sought to counter the reputation his enemies had created. He attempted to write without seeming self-interested or appearing to publicly campaign, which would be considered ungentlemanly at the time. The young republic was an experimental government with few standing rules, and great emphasis was placed on the public reputation of its "worthiest" men. Politics was high drama masquerading as dispassionate adherence to traditional concepts of reason and virtue.

In order to speak in reasonable and virtuous terms while conveying an emotional message, Jefferson addressed Gerry forthrightly. "I shall make to you a profession of my political faith," he said, hoping that his personal touch, his sincere and friendly tone, would defeat "calumny." It was a test of the power of literary sentiment to translate into political authority, something at which Jefferson had masterfully succeeded when he produced a Declaration that brought thirteen distinct colonies—New England and the South alike—into a harmonious union.

And so he listed his principles, just as he had listed the colonies' common grievances in 1776: "I do, then, with sincere zeal, wish an inviolable preservation of our federal constitution." So much for those who asserted that Jefferson did not approve its orderly features. "I am opposed to monarchising it's features ... with a view to conciliate a first transition to a President & Senate for life, & from that to a hereditary tenure of these offices, & thus to worm out the elective principle." This was Jefferson's real fear of the direction in which the Hamiltonians would take the United States if given free reign.

He went on to outline a complete political program that he expected Gerry to approve, one that was liberal in the context of its day. Jefferson was staunchest in his support of freedom of the press, which was just then under attack. "And I am for encouraging the progress of science in all it's branches; and not for raising a hue and cry against the sacred name of philosophy." Here he was referring to the religious conservatives who considered Jefferson's uncensored love of knowledge a rejection of spiritual life. He welcomed these enemies, for to Jefferson they would ridiculously "go backwards instead of forwards to look for improvement; to believe that government, religion, morality, & every other science were the highest perfection in ages of the darkest ignorance."

As to the delicate matter of the French Revolution, so disruptive to Europe, so divisive in America, Jefferson continued to offer his unabashed opinions, which he trusted his correspondent would find entirely reasonable:

> *I was a sincere well-wisher to the success of the French revolution, and still wish it may end in the establishment of a free & well-ordered republic; but I have not been insensible under the atrocious depredations they have committed on our commerce. The first object of my heart is my own country. In that is embarked my family, my fortune, & my own existence.*

He was proclaiming himself an American patriot and hoping to excite Gerry's sympathetic response to the beating of his breast. "These, my friend, are my principles," Jefferson concluded the thought, presuming, "I know there is not one of them which is not yours also." Even if these two men had political differences that channeled them into competing political parties, Jefferson implied, they had much more in common than in opposition.

Eighteenth-century letters, by definition, provided the means to overcome distance. They promoted a civilized code of conduct, enabling the exchange of ideas and feelings in a refined and carefully constituted forum. Letters also created expectations. Thus in writing Gerry, Jefferson fulfilled a personal promise while eliciting a new one: "When I sat down to answer your letter," he attested, "but two things presented themselves; either to say nothing or every thing; for half confidences are not in my character. I could not hesitate which was due to you. I have unbosomed myself fully; & it will certainly be highly gratifying if I receive like confidence from you."

The letter evidently impressed its recipient. After Jefferson defeated the incumbent Adams and became president, Elbridge Gerry gradually changed party affiliation. In 1812, he joined James Madison's ticket and served as vice president of the United States until his death in 1814.

Speech

OF
THOMAS JEFFERSON,

PRESIDENT of the UNITED STATES—*delivered at his* INAUGURATION, *March* 4, 1801.

Friends & Fellow-Citizens,

CALLED upon to undertake the duties of the first executive office of our country, I avail myself of the presence of that portion of my fellow-citizens which is here assembled, to express my grateful thanks for the favour with which they have been pleased to look towards me, to declare a sincere consciousness that the task is above my talents, and that I approach it with those anxious and awful presentiments, which the greatness of the charge, and the weakness of my powers so justly inspire. A rising nation, spread over a wide and fruitful land, traversing all the seas with the rich productions of their industry, engaged in commerce with nations who feel power and forget right; advancing rapidly to destinies beyond the reach of mortal eye; when I contemplate these transcendant objects, and see the honor, the happiness and the hopes of this beloved country, committed to the issue and the auspices of this day, I shrink from the contemplation, and humble myself before the magnitude of the undertaking. Utterly, indeed, should I despair, did not the presence of many, whom I here see, remind me, that in the other high authorities, provided by our Constitution, I shall find resources of wisdom, of virtue, and of zeal, on which to rely under all difficulties. To you, then, gentlemen, who are charged with the sovereign functions of legislation, and to those associated with you, I look with encouragement for that guidance and support which may enable us to steer with safety the vessel in which we are all embarked, amidst the conflicting elements of a troubled world.

During the contest of opinion through which we have passed, the animation of discussions and of exertions has sometimes worn an aspect which might impose on strangers unused to think freely, and to speak and to write what they think; but this being now decided by the voice of the nation, announced according to the rules of the Constitution, all will, of course, arrange themselves under the will of the law, and unite in common efforts for the common good. All too will bear in mind this sacred principle, that though the will of the majority is in all cases to prevail, that will to be rightful must be reasonable; that the minority possess their equal rights, which equal laws must protect, and to violate would be oppression. Let us, then, fellow-citizens, unite with one heart and one mind, let us restore to social intercourse that harmony and affection, without which liberty, and even life itself, are but dreary things. And let us reflect that having banished from our land that religious intolerance, under which mankind so long bled and suffered, we have yet gained little, if we countenance a political intolerance, as despotic, as wicked, and capable of as bitter and bloody persecutions. During the throes and convulsions of the ancient world, during the agonizing spasms of infuriated man, seeking through blood and slaughter his long lost liberty, it was not wonderful that the agitation of the billows should reach even this distant and peaceful shore; that this should be more felt and feared by some, and less by others; and should divide opinions as to measures of safety; but every difference of opinion is not a difference of principle. We have called by different names brethren of the same principle.—*We are* ALL *Republicans*—*We are* ALL *Federalists*. If there be any among us who would dissolve this union, or change its republican form, let them stand undisturbed as monuments of the safety with which error of opinion may be tolerated, where reason is left free to combat it. I know indeed that some honest men fear that a republican government cannot be strong; that this government is not strong enough. But would the honest patriot, in the full tide of successful experiment, abandon a government which has so far kept us free and firm, on the theoretic and visionary fear, that this government, the world's best hope, may, by possibility, want energy to preserve itself? I trust not. I believe this, on the contrary, the strongest government on earth. I believe it the only one, where every man, at the call of the law, would fly to the standard of the law, and would meet invasions of the public order as his own personal concern.—Sometimes it is said that man cannot be trusted with the government of himself. Can he then be trusted with the government of others? Or have we found angels, in the form of kings, to govern him? Let history answer this question.

Let us then, with courage and confidence, pursue our own federal and republican principles; our attachment to union and representative government. Kindly separated by nature and a wide ocean, from the exterminating havoc of one quarter of the globe: too high-minded to endure the degradations of the others, possessing a chosen country, with room enough for our descendants to the thousandth and thousandth generation; entertaining a due sense of our equal right to the use of our own faculties, to the acquisitions of our own industry, to honor and confidence from our fellow-citizens; resulting not from birth, but from our actions and their sense of them; enlightened by a benign religion, professed indeed, and practised in various forms, yet all of them inculcating honesty, truth, temperance, gratitude and the love of man; acknowledging and adoring an over-ruling Providence, which, by all its dispensations, proves, that it delights in the happiness of man here, and his greater happiness hereafter; with all these blessings, what more is necessary to make us a happy and a prosperous people? Still one thing more, fellow-citizens, a wise and frugal government, which shall restrain men from injuring one another, shall leave them otherwise free to regulate their own pursuits of industry and improvement, and shall not take from the mouth of labour the bread it has earned. This is the sum of good government; and this is necessary to close the circle of our felicities.

About to enter, fellow-citizens, on the exercise of duties which comprehend every thing dear and valuable to you, it is proper you should understand what I deem the essential principles of our government, and, consequently, those which ought to shape its administration. I will comprefs them within the narrowest compass they will bear, stating the general principle, but not all its limitations.—Equal and exact justice to all men, of whatever state or persuasion, religious or political! Peace, commerce and honest friendship with all nations, entangling alliances with none;—the support of the state governments in all their rights, as the most competent administrations for our domestic concerns, and the surest bulwarks against anti-republican tendencies; the preservation of the general government in its whole constitutional vigor, as the sheet anchor of our peace at home, and safety abroad;—a jealous care of the right of election by the people, a mild and safe corrective of abuses which are lopped by the sword of revolution, where peaceable remedies are unprovided;—absolute acquiescence in the decisions of the majority, the vital principle of republics, from which is no appeal but to force, the vital principle and immediate parent of despotism;—a well disciplined militia, our best reliance in peace, and for the first moments of war, till regulars may relieve them; the supremacy of the civil over the military authority;—œconomy in the public expence, that labour may be lightly burthened;—the honest payment of our debts, and sacred preservation of the public faith; encouragement of agriculture, and of commerce as its hand-maid;—the diffusion of information, and arraignment of all abuses at the bar of the public reason ;—freedom of religion ; freedom of the press; and freedom of the person, under the protection of the Habeas Corpus :—and trial by juries impartially selected.—These principles form the bright constellation, which has gone before us and guided our steps through an age of revolution and reformation. The wisdom of our sages, and blood of our heroes, have been devoted to their attainment. They should be the creed of our political faith; the text of civic instruction; the touch-stone by which to try the services of those we trust; and should we wander from them in moments of error or of alarm, let us hasten to retrace our steps, and to regain the road which alone leads to peace, liberty and safety.

I repair, then, fellow-citizens, to the post, you have assigned me. With experience enough in subordinate offices, to have seen the difficulties of this, the greatest of all, I have learnt to expect that it will rarely fall to the lot of imperfect man to retire from this station with the reputation and favour which bring him into it. Without pretensions to that confidence which you reposed in our first and greatest revolutionary character, whose pre-eminent services had entitled him to the first place in his country's love, and destined for him the fairest page in the volume of faithful history, I ask so much confidence only, as may give firmness and effect to the legal administration of your affairs. I shall often go wrong through defect of judgment. When right, I shall often be thought wrong by those whose positions will not command a view of the whole ground. I ask your indulgence for my own errors, which will never be intentional; and your support against the errors of others, who may condemn what they would not, if seen in all its parts. The approbation implied by your suffrage, is a great consolation to me for the past; and my future solicitude will be, to retain the good opinion of those who have bestowed it in advance, to conciliate that of others, by doing them all the good in my power, and to be instrumental to the happiness and freedom of all.

Relying then, on the patronage of your good will, I advance with obedience to the work, *ready to retire from it whenever you become sensible how much better choices it is in your power to make.* And may that infinite power, which rules the destinies of the Universe, lead our councils to what is best, and give them a favourable issue for your peace and prosperity.

W. PECHIN—PRINT.

Silk broadside showing Thomas Jefferson's first inaugural address (courtesy of Charles Bell Papers, Swen Library, College of William and Mary)

Chapter Six

FIRST INAUGURAL ADDRESS

A rising nation, spread over a wide and fruitful land, traversing all the seas with the rich productions of their industry, engaged in commerce with nations who feel power and forget right, advancing rapidly to destinies beyond the reach of mortal eye—when I contemplate these transcendent objects, and see the honor, the happiness, and the hopes of this beloved country, I shrink from the contemplation, and humble myself before the magnitude of the undertaking.[26]

The above words, spoken in the Senate chamber on March 4, 1801, and widely printed thereafter, crystallize Jeffersonian awe and optimism. They combine an Enlightenment-age appreciation for the sublime effects of nature with the incoming president's nationalistic faith in the good attainable through American territorial expansion. Although politics was Jefferson's "trade" and what he is best known for, he considered himself most suited to engage with the public as a gentleman thinker and natural philosopher. Therefore, as he combined his sentimental vision of friendship with his prescription for republicanism, he used a vocabulary drawn from literary and philosophical worlds to merge the two.

His political enemies, interpreting the Jeffersonian idiom in their own way, called the president an "airy philosopher," fearing that he was not enough of a realist to function as a national executive. In this, Jefferson proved his detractors much mistaken, for he became one of the boldest executives who ever held the highest office.

His first inaugural address caused many on both sides of the political divide to pause. He was the first United States president to be inaugurated in

Washington, D.C., but his sentiment-filled inaugural address reverberated in the still highly politicized atmosphere of Philadelphia. It was said (perhaps with exaggerated optimism) that men who had shunned one another were inspired to converse again. His friend and fellow Declaration signer Dr. Benjamin Rush wrote him, "Your character as a philosopher and friend of mankind predominates so much more in my mind over that of your new station.... You have opened a new era."[27]

We need to look both at the sentimental vision of friendship and at the general prescription for republicanism in order to understand Jefferson's united philosophy of government. For his was indeed an idealistic formula, requiring principles more usually applied to friendship to form the foundation of a government. He called for a generous and sympathetic use of power, and the literary style of his private correspondence and presidential texts fulfills this purpose of reaching toward social harmony. Jefferson was the first president to employ this strategy, but he was certainly not the last.

As the Declaration of Independence demonstrates, Jefferson understood the potential for language to express the heartfelt yearnings of a collective people, that is, for language to unite people separated by distance or dissimilarity. As America grew and absorbed new waves of immigrants, it faced the challenge of creating a unified culture. Jefferson recognized that language could combine many interests into one common interest. In the Declaration, Jefferson accomplished this by creating phrases of positive assent such as "life, liberty, and the pursuit of happiness," as well as by identifying the patriots' common fear of their land being "exposed to all the dangers of invasion from without and convulsions within." As president, he faced no immediate crisis comparable to that of foreign invasion, and he had only to emphasize the positive.

In the opening sequence of his first inaugural address, Jefferson minimized himself in the composition ("I shrink from the contemplation") in order to highlight the greatness of something larger than personal achievement: America. "A rising nation," young, healthy, and growing, "spread over a wide and fruitful land," was even at this time, in its infancy, "traversing all the seas." Seagoing commerce represented dynamic possibility in 1801; the Jeffersonian mindset embraced the possibility that when American ships docked at foreign ports, the sailors and merchants could export the enthusiasm of a young, open, and hopeful country, resuscitating the older, crowded, corrupted, and war-torn civilizations in Europe and Asia. Several lines later, Jefferson employs the metaphor of the sea to establish the power of Congress to set a republican example for a troubled world: "I look with encouragement," he states, "for that guidance and support which may enable us to steer with safety the vessel in which we are all embarked."

In Jefferson's address, these American vessels were heading to "nations who feel power and forget right." Again, he refers to the compassion that Americans were meant to possess, a compassion that other cultures, burdened by monarchical oppression, desperately lacked. All they felt was power. On the other hand, America, pointed ahead to "destinies beyond the reach of mortal eye," appeared to be confidently embracing purposes that he labeled "transcendent."

Indeed, America's energy should now be focused on solidifying virtuous connections. The president explained to his national audience that the recent tumult brought on by party rivalry had not destroyed American principles; rather he avowed that to be American was to be humane and humanistic, and that leadership was sustained by "the consent of the governed," citing the Declaration. To fulfill the Declaration's promise, he launched into his most memorable, and most harmonizing, rhetoric: "every difference of opinion is not a difference of principle," he said. "We have called by different names brethren of the same principle. We are all republicans—we are all federalists."

The significance of this language is so great that we must digress considerably and examine how else the deliberative Jefferson develops his dramatic intent. The explanation entails coming to terms with an unfamiliar way of thinking, the Enlightenment understanding of nervous physiology and moral impulses. Jefferson drew upon this to get his essential point across to the people of his time, and if we are to appreciate his words as his hearers and readers did, we need to make the same linguistic and emotional connections.

Jeffersonian sentiment revolved around a concept of *sympathy* no longer current. In the late eighteenth century, it was widely understood that a natural sympathy coursed through the nerves. It was equally understood that humans possessed generosity from birth as a natural endowment—what today we would probably refer to in genetic terms. This same natural, or nerve-borne, sympathy was believed to be translatable, in a republic, into enlightened policy.

Understandings of the human nervous system reflected not just a potential for positive social change, but explained, too, the chaotic inner life that most Americans experienced. The "thousand natural shocks that flesh is heir to," to borrow from Shakespeare, effectively describes the Enlightenment conception of individual moral struggle and national political struggle. For Jefferson, who wrote in terms of *individual* rights, *individual* will, *individual* promise, and *individual* contributions to the public good, human physiology was integral to his political philosophy; human feeling related to his scientific world as much as to his literary imagination.

In his influential *Essay Concerning the Human Understanding*, John Locke first described the psycho-perceptual system in humans: the human mind, he wrote, received impressions; human feeling was the motion of nerve fibers. These fibers set off tremors, which in turn affected the human conscience; thus morals were inseparable from innate physiology. The literary name for this physiological phenomenon was sensibility. Pains, pleasure, moral sense—all of these concepts were interconnected. Unseen interior forces were the essence of life: when touched or stimulated, the nerves transmitted "impressions" to the soul.

Sensibility was to the revolutionaries what Darwin or Freud was to Americans of a later period. Enlightenment thought paid homage to sensibility as much as it did to reason. Accordingly, following the physiological metaphor, government transmitted impressions to the "body politic" through legislation, and the issuance of legislative impressions produced either painful or pleasurable sensations; policy was either just or unjust, and invariably had moral consequences.[28]

So now we are, in a way, back in Jefferson's world, viscerally feeling the words as his audience did, understanding that he chose his metaphors carefully in order to have a conscious effect or to tap into the nervous constitution. In his first inaugural address, as he led up to his harmonizing prescription "We are all republicans—we are all federalists," he first defined public "harmony" as public "affection." His design for the future was simple: "Let us, then, fellow citizens, unite with one heart and one mind. Let us restore to social intercourse that harmony and affection without which liberty and even life itself are but dreary things." In a section of the Declaration removed by his Congressional editors, Jefferson condemned crown appointees as "disturbers of our harmony." Recall, too, his letters to daughters Martha and Maria, invoking the central goal of one's life in terms of "harmony and affection." He would have the nation's goal be the same.

But dangers still lurked, and so he alerted the American people to the nervous condition into which America could devolve if the political experiment failed. He feared a return to unenlightened impulses of the past, especially the European past, in which religious intolerance brought on destructive wars:

> *Let us reflect that having banished from our land that religious intolerance under which mankind so long bled and suffered, we have gained little if we countenance a political intolerance as despotic, as wicked, as capable of bitter and bloody persecutions. During the throes and convulsions of the ancient world, during the agonizing spasms of infuriated man, seeking through blood and slaughter his long-lost liberty, it was not wonderful that the agitation of the billows should reach even this distant and peaceful shore; that this should be more felt and feared by some and less by others; that this should divide opinions as to measures of safety.*

This long passage immediately precedes the call to put aside partisanship long enough to recognize common principles, or the common pursuit of social harmony. It is an exhortation at once hopeful and cautionary, and cast in language of nervous sensibility: what could be more disruptive to the balance of nerves than to re-encounter the "throes and convulsions" that beset antiquity? Once more, Jefferson is employing the word *convulsions* to weigh against the pursuit of domestic peace. In the Declaration he held the king responsible for convulsions within the American body politic, for George III had "sent hither swarms of new officers to harass our people and eat out their substance." Now, he urges Americans to avoid revisiting the primitive antagonisms of the ancient world, when the world was forced to endure the "agonizing spasms of infuriated man" to achieve liberty.

Who would wish to endure that again? The enlightened republic was meant to escape the past, to reason through political difficulties, to find "harmony and affection," and to prove that humanity had finally left behind wrenching times of "blood and slaughter." Jefferson urged Americans to grasp their opportunity and to build on their revolutionary spirit. For America was, he said, "the world's best hope."

He was saying, too, that "long-lost liberty," that basic natural right that oppressive governments had systematically stolen over the ages, had been dramatically won back in the American Revolution. And so he would contrast the nerve-wracked past with a healthier, more hopeful present. To Jefferson, the history of the world was a visceral history of "agonizing spasms of infuriated man." The new course of history, in Jefferson's progressive outlook, was marked by the continuous, emotional response of liberty seekers to an unjust political environment. The past was a diseased world in search of health, a violent world in search of peace. The Enlightenment Jefferson believed in was meant to be the culmination of that search.

When he goes on to say, "We are all republicans—we are all federalists," he is saying that a politics in pursuit of "harmony and affection" is succeeding a politics rent by "agonizing spasms." Emotional harmony will be brought into the body politic by way of "balanced nerves," applying an eighteenth-century understanding of physiology to a moral realm. For without "harmony and affection," at least to Jefferson, "liberty and even life itself are but dreary things."

If we take Jefferson at his word, angry partisan language only served to impair the political nervous system. And yet, here is the irony of it: *Jefferson was an angry partisan.* His private communications with political allies do not show him as a harmonizer, but expose him as one who consistently doubts that the two competing parties of his time could coexist. He saw the Federalists not merely as counter-productive but as abrasive and ultimately incompatible with America. He vowed to wear them down through policies that revealed them to be out of touch, and to expose them as an aristocratic or monarchical party that paid only lip service to the idea of representative democracy. He wanted them gone.

Hardened Federalists regarded Jefferson as outwardly soft and inwardly duplicitous. Because education in this era was not as widespread as it is now, and because settlements were smaller and far more spread apart, many of the found-ers feared democratization. They feared entrusting power to those outside elite circles, and in President Jefferson's language of inclusiveness they heard a dema-gogue pandering to the untrustworthy masses. He was, in the words of one lead-ing Federalist, "a dish of skim milk, curdling at the head of the nation." Just as he saw their methods as covetous and corrupt, they saw his populist pronouncements as destabilizing and even anarchic.

Then how should we read the powerful prose of his first inaugural address? Do we placate ourselves by thinking that he was merely human, and that like all humans, his principles were simply better than he was? In the same way that we try to understand Jefferson the slave owner as an essentially humane man trapped in an utterly inhumane system, should we perceive his damning of the Federalist party as the reaction of one who simply could not escape the demanding concerns and dominant personalities of his generation? These are questions for each gen-eration to answer, questions on which no historian can effectively rule. Jefferson tried to project moral improvement, but like any emotionally complex person, he is morally incomplete.

Perhaps what Jefferson should have done, but of course could not have done in his time, was to acknowledge the two faces of political rhetoric: "We are all harmonizers, we are all extremists." Suffice it to say that Jefferson—the historic Jefferson, not the enduringly eloquent writer Jefferson—was partisan and paro-chial. Those who decry him for owning slaves certainly understand this. He was not transcendent. But if he was pandering to his constituency and pandering to us, his posterity, in the first inaugural address, he has done a convincing job of it. He knew how to reach deep with his words, how to tap into feeling, and how to activate sense and arouse sensibility.

Therefore, the best way to encounter Jefferson is by examining what he studied, and trying to work from the body of knowledge available to him—not that available to us. In the age of sensibility, as we have seen here, the sensible part of the body that transmitted impressions to the soul made the nervous sys-tem mysterious, dramatic, and suggestive of soulful power and purpose. Jefferson wrote with a passionate pen, a "nervous" pen, to use the language of the eighteenth century. The adjective *nervous* meant active, vigorous, in the sense of masculine vigor and activity. Nerve and vigor made Jefferson a great humanist. Nerve and vigor are why his words continue to resonate even today.

His hope described America's idealized image of itself. He, more than anyone else of that founding generation, gave this country a set of moral values to realize. So when Jefferson pronounced his deepest faith, it was in the language of the heart to conquer prejudice. "Let us, then, fellow citizens, unite with one heart and one mind" in order to "restore harmony and affection," defining American optimism for the ages. His restorative idiom was there for Lincoln to draw upon at Gettysburg threescore and two years later.

All of these reasons demonstrate why Jefferson's first inaugural address probably remains the most "Jeffersonian" of all of his compositions and deserves our most careful scrutiny. It presents Jeffersonian prose in the best light, perhaps even more than the celebrated Declaration of Independence, which was meant to disrupt and inflame passions while making a legal case, whereas the inaugural address was meant to project pure "affection." North and South were already eyeing each other suspiciously. The president spoke, presciently, as it turns out, on behalf of union and unity.

The citizens whom Jefferson addressed on March 4, 1801, appreciated his dramatic use of language and his nervous, vigorous, rhetorical style, because they lived with personal crises almost daily. Their letters invariably carried news of illness, infant mortality, mothers dying after difficult births, cities reduced by yellow fever, influenza, malaria, or smallpox. The emotional reality the revolutionary generation knew was painful in ways we can no longer feel. They conceived of immortality in the form of a representative government assuring them of continued liberty.

That is why throughout his life, in his personal as well as his more renowned public documents, Jefferson wrote to convey friendship, consolation, trust, sincerity—the investment of heart. He used language to touch others so effectively that they believed they were striving together with him to create an orderly, stable society—contrary to what his political enemies fearfully projected he would do. His presidency helped to sustain the public order while offering an unprecedented degree of personal liberty.

He knew what history taught, that those who took part in political life were generally led to covet power and position. But he somehow believed that in America the impulse to live free would lead a revolutionary people to exercise humane power, power that was indistinguishable from zealous good will.

Joseph Priestley *(courtesy of the Burndy Library, Dibner Institute for the History of Science and Technology, Cambridge, Massachusetts.)*

Chapter Seven

DEFENDING A VISION

As the storm is now subsiding, and the horizon becoming serene, it is pleasant to consider the phenomenon with attention. We can no longer say there is nothing new under the sun. For this whole chapter in the history of man is new. The great extent of our Republic is new. It's sparse habitation is new. The mighty wave of public opinion which has rolled over it is new.[29]

On March 21, 1801, just seventeen days after delivering his first inaugural address, Jefferson wrote to Dr. Joseph Priestley, a political ally and a man of scientific genius whom the president deeply respected. A true virtuoso, Priestley was born in England in 1733, discovered oxygen in 1774, and as a clergyman authored his *History of the Corruptions of Christianity* in 1782. In this book, he propounded what Jefferson accepted as a sensible balance between reason and faith: early Christian practices were simple and sublime, a system of morals subsequently corrupted by complex and useless rituals of worship. Jefferson inferred from Priestley's work that the clerical caste in New England, who thumped their fists from the pulpit and vilified Jefferson, were bent on compelling submission, and in their vindictiveness bore no resemblance to the original Christians.

In September 1800, Jefferson wrote the religious patriot and educator Dr. Benjamin Rush the sonorous words that now wrap around the Jefferson Memorial in Washington, "I have sworn upon the altar of God, eternal hostility to every form of tyranny over the mind of man," but it was Dr. Priestley's influential book that gave Jefferson the impetus to speak out against clerical bigotry as he saw it. Priestley believed in divine revelation through the Bible, but he asserted that Jesus was human, albeit a human with a divine role. Jefferson, too, was to write that he found in Jesus every "human" excellence.

How, then, did the English theologian who had discovered oxygen end up in America as a Jeffersonian? In 1790, the year after the Bastille fell, Priestley openly expressed sympathy for the French Revolution—a highly unpopular position to adopt in England. Mobs burned down his church. He held on as long as he felt safe, but in 1794 Priestley became a refugee, sailing to Philadelphia, where he was welcomed with open arms into the American Philosophical Society, founded by the late Benjamin Franklin in 1743, the year of Jefferson's birth. Jefferson served as president of the society concurrent with his terms as vice president and president of the United States; he had ample opportunity to communicate with Priestley on various scientific, religious, and political subjects of mutual interest and concern.

Thus, Jefferson wrote to a kindred spirit during the first weeks of his presidency. "Yours is one of the few lives precious to mankind," the president praised. Again railing against the clerics whose voices so loudly attacked him, Jefferson continued, "What an effort, my dear Sir, of bigotry in Politics & Religion have we gone through! The barbarians really flattered themselves they should be able to bring back the time of Vandalism, when ignorance put every thing into the hands of power & priestcraft."

Yet Jefferson did not write merely to lash out at those against him: "Our countrymen have recovered from the alarm," he relaxed. "Science & honesty are replaced on their high ground; and you my dear Sir, as their great apostle, are on it's pinnacle." As president, Jefferson promised good laws and civil rights to Priestley, a man hounded by those who held the Alien Act over his head.

Thus the president could claim to have effected a massive change in the tenor of government, what in later years he himself would refer to as the "Revolution of 1800." He had entered office, as he put it, with "the country entirely in the enemies hands," yet he believed he left the presidency having ended the "English," or Hamiltonian, system, securing constitutional liberties through a fair election. This feeling of triumph led Jefferson to write to Priestley of the sudden meteorological shift: "As the storm is now subsiding, and the horizon becoming serene, it is pleasant to consider the phenomenon with attention. We can no longer say there is nothing new under the sun...."

Almost breathlessly, Jefferson pronounced the end of the political storm unleashed by the Federalists of 1798, which had threatened the very foundation of the republic. "The order & good sense displayed in this recovery from delusion, and in the momentous crisis which lately arose, really bespeak a strength of character in our nation which augurs well for the duration of our Republic." One can almost imagine Jefferson puckishly winking as he expressed his relief to Priestley: "But I have got into a long disquisition on politics, when I only meant to express my sympathy in the state of your health...."

For his part, Priestley, the "rational Christian," or Unitarian, wrote to an English friend in February 1802 that after his first year in office Jefferson had proven that republicanism was practicable: "He is every thing that the friends of liberty can wish." And in 1804, as he sensed his own decline, Priestley wrote another of the president's philosophic friends, "Tell Mr. Jefferson that I think myself happy to have lived so long under his excellent administration; and that I have a prospect of dying in it. It is, I am confident, the best on the face of the earth, and yet I hope to rise to some thing more excellent still." Only days later, still annotating the Old and New Testaments, Joseph Priestley died peacefully at his home in Northumberland, Pennsylvania.

Jefferson identified strongly with Priestley's fight against established dogmas, and Priestley related to Jefferson's quarrel with political elitism. Much like today, theirs was a time when private sentiments often merged with national politics, and when the "reason" of a religious scientist could present, for some, a profound moral challenge. In noting his "affectionate respect" for Priestley, Jefferson, who also understood love and loss and the value of the intellectually active life, wrote a few years later: "In religion, in politics, in physics, no man has rendered more service." As to the value of their friendship, Jefferson penned: "I revered the character of no man living more than his."

Washington June 25, 1804

Your letter, my dear friend, of the 25th ult. is a new proof of the goodness of your heart, and the part you take in my loss marks an affectionate concern for the greatness of it. it is great indeed. others may lose of their abundance, but I, of my want, have lost even the half of what I had. my evening prospects now hang on the slender thread of a single life. perhaps I may be destined to see even this last cord of parental affection broken! the hope with which I had looked forward to the moment, when resigning public cares to younger hands I was to retire to that domestic comfort from which the last great step is to be taken, is fearfully blighted. when you and I look out on the country over which we have passed, under all the inspiring energies of health and hope what a field of slaughter does it exhibit. where are all the friends who entered it with us? as if pursued by the havoc of war, they are strowed by the way, some earlier, some later, and scarce a few stragglers remain to count the numbers fallen, and to mark yet by their own fall the last footsteps of their party. is it a desireable thing to bear up thro' the heat of the action, to witness the death of all our companions, and merely be the last victim? I doubt it. we have however the traveller's consolation. every step shortens the distance we have to go; the end of our journey is in sight, the bed wherein we are to rest, and to rise in the midst of the friends we have lost. 'we sorrow not then as others who have no hope,' but look forward to the day which 'joins us to the great majority.' but whatever is to be our destiny, wisdom, as well as duty, dictates that we should acquiesce in the will of him whose it is to give and to take away, and be contented in the enjoyment of those who are still permitted to be with us. of those connected by blood the number does not depend on us, but friends we have if we have merited them. those of our earliest years stand nearest in our affections, but in this too you and I have been unlucky. of our college friends (and they are the dearest)

Governor Page

Jefferson to John Page, June 25, 1804 (image enhanced; courtesy of the Library of Congress.)

Chapter Eight

A LIFELONG FRIENDSHIP

When you and I look out on the country over which we have passed, what
a field of slaughter does it exhibit. Where are all the friends who entered it
with us, under all the inspiring energies of health and hope? As if pursued
by the havoc of war, they are strewed by the way, some earlier, some later,
and scarce a few straglers remain to count the numbers fallen, and to mark
yet by their own fall the last footsteps of their party.[30]

Thomas Jefferson's friendship with the elder Joseph Priestley endured one decade, from the time of Priestley's arrival in America until his death. Jefferson's friendship with John Page, however, lasted nearly half a century.

A slender, soft-spoken, seventeen-year-old Jefferson first met Page in 1760 as they began their studies together at the College of William and Mary. They shared teenage secrets, and later grew to be political allies in momentous times. Page's family was the wealthier of the two; he inherited an estate called Rosewell in the established, populous Virginia Tidewater. Jefferson was from Albemarle County in the Virginia Piedmont and, relatively speaking, a child of the frontier.

Page later wrote that no one in their college class studied as long and hard as Jefferson. "I was too sociable, and fond of the conversation of my friends," Page acknowledged. But Jefferson "could tear himself away from his dearest friends, to fly to his studies." The intellectually adventuresome duo shared an interest in astronomy. One time in 1770, while Jefferson was back in Albemarle and Page was proving the less reliable correspondent, Jefferson joked in a letter to his friend, "Why the devil don't you write? But I suppose you are always in the moon, or some of the planetary regions. I mean you are there in idea, and unless you mend, you shall have my consent to be there de facto."[31]

The earliest Jefferson-Page correspondence reveals future revolutionaries in their uninitiated state, projecting from books what the world was like, and imagining the grand lessons they would learn as their social roles evolved. Speculating on the pursuit of happiness in 1763, an agitated twenty-year-old Jefferson lamented:

> *Perfect happiness I beleive was never intended by the deity to be the lot of any one of his creatures.... The most fortunate of us all in our journey through life frequently meet with calamities and misfortunes which may greatly afflict us; and to fortify our minds against the attacks of these calamities and misfortunes should be one of the principal studies and endeavors of our lives.*[32]

Consciously or not, he was steeling himself for a life of struggle, to which he would grow habituated as he took a more active interest in political affairs. Without friendship, sustained by letter writing, he would never have succeeded in politics to the same degree.

Exaggerating the importance of their confidences, Jefferson proposed around this same time to encode letters that might miscarry. "We must fall on some scheme of communicating our thoughts to each other, which shall be totally unintelligible to every one but ourselves."[33] We can conclude from this that Jefferson was sensitive about revealing his private thoughts and suspicious about others' prying eyes.

When Jefferson attended the Continental Congress in Philadelphia in 1775, he continued to keep in close touch with Page, now an active participant in the Virginia Committee of Safety, which was monitoring the conduct of Tories and crown officials. "I can declare without boasting," the patriot Page wrote his friend, "that I feel such Indignation against the Authors of our Grievances and the Scoundrel Pirates in our Rivers and Such Concern for the Public at large that I have not and can not think of my own puny Person and insignificant Affairs." Jefferson was in a position to do something about what so bothered his friend: "For God's sake," Page implored, "declare the Colonies independent at once, and save us from ruin." As we well know, Jefferson obliged.[34]

Amid the Revolution in the contest for governor of Virginia in 1779, Jefferson and Page were placed in opposition to one another. Though at that time Page was serving as lieutenant governor, Jefferson secured more votes in the state assembly and won the executive job; but he would do nothing to invite a rupture in their friendship. Perceiving the closeness of the vote (sixty-seven to sixty-one), Jefferson wrote the unsuccessful candidate, "the difference in number which decided between us was too insignificant to give you a pain or me a pleasure [had] our dispositions towards each other been such as to have admitted those sensations." When Page was obliged to leave the Virginia capital suddenly and was thus unable to congratulate Jefferson properly, he left a note: "I have such Confidence in your good Opinion of my Heart that were it not for the World who may put a wrong Construction on my Conduct I should scarcely trouble you with this Apology." Jefferson answered immediately: "I know you too well to need an apology for any thing you do.... As this is the first, so I hope it will be the last instance of ceremony between us." The letter was signed, "Your affectionate friend."[35]

Their religious views differed dramatically. Page was an ardent supporter of the Episcopal Church and strove for state support; Jefferson focused his attention on systematizing the separation of church and state. Yet the very public nature of such debate did not diminish the fraternal feelings that connected the two men. In their letters they brought up their differences in mild and indulgent tones. Jefferson wrote quite unsympathetically to Madison, who very much shared his religious views: "I am glad the Episcopalians have again shewn their teeth and fangs. The dissenters had almost forgotten them."[36] He would never have displayed such disregard for heartfelt sentiments to Page directly, and in later years even quoted the *Book of Common Prayer* to an ailing Page. Strong-minded, even uncompromising in his politics, Jefferson tried to soften every disagreement with the generous sentiments his quill pen could produce. Some might call this duplicitous, though it also seems a natural and utterly humane response.

John Page, for his part, stood by Jefferson throughout his struggle to defeat Hamilton and the Federalists. As a member of the United States Congress from 1789 to 1797, he worked closely with the Democratic-Republicans, and he helped to elect Jefferson president in 1800. Page was then elected governor of Virginia, a post he held from 1802 to 1805.

Jefferson would no doubt say, however, that Page did him the most good as a close personal friend. In their time, death was always imminent. People recognized that medicine rarely did much good, and they indulged their anguished feelings without becoming absorbed in self-pity upon experiencing the inevitable loss of loved ones; friendship assisted the grieving process. So many letters announced and mourned the passing of friends and relatives—in 1788, for example, Page wrote a letter to Jefferson in Paris that not only disclosed the death of his own wife after "a long Indisposition," but also listed five others among their close acquaintances who had suffered comparable losses. Writing released tension; friends provided an imaginative communion.

Jefferson lost his father at fourteen, his favorite sister, Jane, when he was twenty-two, his close friend and brother-in-law Dabney Carr just as he turned thirty, and his own wife when he was thirty-nine and she just thirty-three. In the spring of 1804, his fragile younger daughter, Maria, died after a difficult childbirth much like that which her mother had proven unable to endure in 1782. Jefferson, sixty-two and nearing the end of his first term as president, did not handle it well. His surviving daughter, Martha, found her father at home after Maria's funeral, alone, and uncharacteristically clutching a Bible.

Learning of Maria's untimely death, John Page wrote a fine letter of condolence to the grieving father. Jefferson, in his earnest reply, produced one of the most touching and nostalgic of his thousands of personal letters. It began: "Your letter, my dear friend, of the 25th ult. is a new proof of the goodness of your heart, and the part you take in my loss marks an affectionate concern for the greatness of it. It is great indeed." Jefferson's words are starkly revealing; unlike the "Head and Heart" dialogue, the words are not contrived, but moving in their simplicity.

He continued: "Others may lose of their abundance, but I, of my want, have lost even the half of what I had. My evening prospects hang on the slender thread of a single life [Martha's]. Perhaps I may be destined to see even this last cord of parental affection broken!" Again, the language is simple and direct. And how striking for Jefferson to disclose his fear of losing the indomitable Martha, destined to be the mother of eleven children; it had been two months since Maria's death, but his torment still dulled his usual capacity to adorn language.

His future was indelibly altered, and Jefferson felt condemned to mourn. "The hope with which I had looked forward to the moment, when resigning public cares to younger hands, I was to retire to that domestic comfort from which the last great step is to be taken, is fearfully blighted." Interestingly, he uses "blighted," a word associated with fertility; in his mind, the passage of time has become a slow and sinking process, recognizing decay, death, and winter's frigid sleep. And so he turns to acknowledge that stage of life that he and Page at that moment share:

> When you and I look out on the country over which we have passed, what a field of slaughter does it exhibit. Where are all the friends who entered it with us, under all the inspiring energies of health and hope? As if pursued by the havoc of war, they are strewed by the way, some earlier, some later, and scarce a few straglers remain to count the numbers fallen, and to mark yet by their own fall the last footsteps of their party.

These are the magnificent words that enrich a friendship, the largely uncensored plaint of a human being who has witnessed more struggle (so much of it self-contained) than the vast majority of his fellows. He has come to ponder, with a poet's determination—as a tragic figure might do—whether the old zest for life is in any way retrievable. He is certain that life offers little that is secure. If all must soon end, how does a man of his age overcome the tendency to see life as a sad waiting game? For this, Jefferson has no good answer.

It is interesting, too, that in preparing the letter, Jefferson composed one particular question, very basic and nearly rhetorical. Rendering the course of life metaphorically as "the country over which we have passed," he posed: "Where are all the friends who entered it with us?" Rereading what he had written, he went back and added a potent phrase between lines in tiny script after "us:" "under all the inspiring energies of health and hope." He wanted to intensify the image for Page, and he did so by bringing him back to their hopeful, youthful days of scholarly debate and easy reveries. It was the "energies of health and hope" that had inspired them to seek greatness and to face and ultimately prevail over all forces in their way.

Having achieved so much—national independence, high office, patriarchal authority—one would expect a kind of complacency to have set in; but that is not at all what seems to have occurred. Instead Jefferson has concluded (and he expects that his old friend Page fully understands) that they are like an exhausted army, still on the march, whose comrades have fallen, one after the other. What remains to be anticipated by them, the "few straglers," but the day that "joins us to the great majority"? He is ready now, he says, to "acquiesce in the will of him whose it is to give and to take away." Still sensitive to Page's religious faith, Jefferson as president appears more comfortable with this idiom than he was just a few years earlier when challenging the power of the clerics demanded so much of his political skill. Still, in the end, the meaning of his letter has to do with the meaning of friendship: "friends we have if we have merited them," he says, "those of our earliest years stand nearest in our affections."

Page did not quite survive to the end of Jefferson's second term. In fact, as would be the case with Jefferson, he began his decline in a state of financial distress. In September 1808, Jefferson sought to comfort the afflicted former governor. Page wrote back from his Rosewell estate: "God bless you! then my dear Friend, for your Consolation. *As to Death*, I have long been prepared to meet it.... I am indeed so weak that I am ready to die this Minute, but I must make Efforts to live. & I declare to you my Friend! that no misfortunes[,] no certain approach of death, have I suffered to sink my Spirits." He closed the letter, "That God Almighty may preserve & bless you my beloved Friend, is the fervent Prayer of your old Friend [signed] John Page."[37]

Page died less than a month later, and Jefferson shortly thereafter consigned the burdens of government to his friend and successor, James Madison. He then mustered the spirit to devote his retirement to grandchildren, gardening, and, of course, letter writing.

Thomas Jefferson Randolph *by Charles Wilson Peale, c.1808 (Thomas Jefferson
Foundation, Inc.)*

Chapter Nine

A GRANDFATHER'S GOOD ADVICE

I never saw an instance of one of two disputants convincing the other by argument. I have seen many, on their getting warm, becoming rude, & shooting one another. Conviction is the effect of our own dispassionate reasoning, either in solitude, or weighing within ourselves, dispassionately, what we hear from others.[38]

Jefferson longed for retirement. Just before leaving Washington for Monticello after seeing his successor inaugurated, Jefferson wrote to a French friend, "Within a few days I retire to my family, my books, and farms; and having gained the harbor myself, I shall look on my friends still buffeting the storm with anxiety indeed, but not with envy. Never did a prisoner, released from his chains, feel such relief as I shall on shaking off the shackles of power." He would never cease to have political opinions, nor express his concerns for his country's future; but he had had enough of what he often termed "the boisterous ocean of political passions."

He was accompanied to Madison's inauguration by his eldest grandson and namesake, Thomas Jefferson Randolph, who was sixteen at the time. Jeff, as the grandson was familiarly known, was in school in Philadelphia in 1808–09, where his grandfather had been addressing letters of encouragement and caution. Though Jeff was spoken of critically by his own mother as "indolent[,] impatient of reproof and *at times* irritable," the president imagined him capable of reform and self-discipline. Thus he recommended a routine he thought reasonable, which emphasized the value of writing: after listening to hours of instructors' lessons, he was meant to "commit to writing every evening the substance of the lectures of the day." To do so, Jefferson calculated, would "oblige you to attend closely to what is delivered to recall it to your memory, to understand, and to digest it in the evening; it will fix it in your memory, and enable you to refresh it at any future time…. Then, if once a week you will, in a letter to me, state a synopsis or summary view of the heads of the lectures of the preceding week, it will give me great satisfaction to attend to your progress." Jefferson was, in modern parlance, a micro-managing grandfather.[39]

Aware of the temptations that enticed youth, the president did not wish to come across as merely bookish, old-fashioned, and didactic. So he advanced his argument protectively and sympathetically: "Your situation," he wrote, "thrown at such a distance from us, & alone, cannot but give us all great anxieties for you." While Jeff had been afforded opportunities because of his name, not enough had been done "towards shielding you from the dangers which surround you."

Jefferson was concerned about Jeff's lack of experience in the "wide world." The answer he came up with was the only practical one: self-reliance. On his own, the teenager would have to learn to develop the defensive skills adults used—thoughtfulness and sobriety—while in the company of strangers: "A determination never to do what is wrong, prudence and good humor, will go far towards securing to you the estimation of the world."

So that the teenager realized this was possible, Jefferson used himself as an example.[40] He wrote about his own choices at that age, for he had lost his father at the time he most needed an older man's advice and judgment: "When I recollect that at 14 years of age, the whole care & direction of myself was thrown on myself entirely, without a relation or friend qualified to advise or guide me, and recollect the various sorts of bad company with which I associated from time to time, I am astonished I did not turn off with some of them, & become as worthless to society as they were." Ultimately, he had looked to models of correctness, his professors at William and Mary, and asked himself: "What course … will insure me their approbation?" Instead of going the way of horse racers, card players, and foxhunters, Jefferson had fixed his mind on men of dignity and established character. His "self-catechising habit," as he now called it, had made him "the honest advocate of my country's rights."

There was another, more immediate problem he felt equipped to help his grandson resolve, one in which he, as president, was implicated. Jeff had told his grandfather that he was being taunted by schoolmates who spoke critically of Jefferson's politics—the teenager took it personally. To this, Jefferson responded with rather particular advice concerning the value of a pacific temperament, such as he had tried to exhibit throughout his public career. How to handle being a Jefferson was indeed difficult; he could only suggest that his grandson do what he himself had done. This "good humor" was something he had learned, Jefferson said, from Benjamin Franklin:

> It was one of the rules which, above all, made Doctor Franklin the most amiable of men in society, "never to contradict anybody." If he was urged to announce an opinion, he did it rather by asking questions, as if for information, or by suggesting doubts. When I hear another express an opinion which is not mine, I say to myself, he has a right to his opinion, as I to mine; why should I question it? His error does me no injury.

It was an ideal formulation: in Jefferson's romantic view of the nation, all citizens would adopt the Franklinian maxim. In reality, however, Jefferson conveyed open-mindedness by practicing something he also recommended to his grandson: "politeness … artificial good humor." It was "effectual," he said.

This "artificial good humor" was a cheaper version of the Franklinian virtue, revealing that while Jefferson often wrote in ideal terms (causing his political detractors to see in him the airy philosopher), he actually harbored a rather pragmatic perspective on getting along with others. Was it hypocrisy or merely the detour that one took to maintain civility?

The letter of advice to Thomas Jefferson Randolph, conventional on the surface, in fact tells us much about Jefferson's worldview as it evolved. He was decorous in his use of language. His morals were not as sincere as perhaps he would have preferred them to be. He was, in the end, a moralist who had developed a strategy to survive in the political world, one which he plainly endorsed in the letter to his grandson: "Keep aloof."

Thomas Jefferson *and* John
Adams *by Mather Brown, 1788.*
(Adams portrait courtesy of the
Boston Athenaeum; Jefferson
portrait courtesy of the National
Portrait Gallery, Smithsonian
Institution.)

Chapter Ten

THE EX-PRESIDENTS

There is a ripeness of time for death, regarding others as well as ourselves, when it is reasonable we should drop off, and make room for another growth. When we have lived our generation out, we should not wish to encroach on another.[41]

There is perhaps no more precious or appealing collection of correspondence between any two American statesmen than the fourteen years of seemingly random speculations and utterly familiar sentiments, which were scratched onto paper, folded, addressed, sealed with wax, and sent through the mail between Charlottesville, Virginia, and Quincy, Massachusetts. From 1812 until their well-coordinated deaths on July 4, 1826, Thomas Jefferson and John Adams wrote a long series of vigorous, mindful, sociable, and at times academic letters, for which history is much the richer.

The fascinating part of all this is that neither man expected that they would ever resume their once-close bond. The two had stopped speaking to one another in 1801 after Jefferson unseated Adams as president. Political division, it seemed, had doomed the former friends, one a tall, thin, and quiet southerner, the other a short, stout, and combative northerner. They had met in the Continental Congress and had remained on intimate terms for years after the Revolution, overlapping in Paris when both served the United States in diplomatic roles. In old age they retrieved the animating spirit of those years, reminiscing about the halcyon days of the struggle to conceive a nation, while querying each other about classical literature, contemporary politics, religion, and more. Their minds never rested; their youthful spirits never faded.

How they recovered their lost friendship is a tale in itself. After Jefferson retired from politics in 1809, Dr. Benjamin Rush of Philadelphia, a signer of the Declaration and a friend to both men, engineered a friendly scheme. He had had a dream, he wrote to Adams, in which the second and third presidents magnanimously renewed their friendship and carried on years of correspondence. The proud, candid Adams wrote back to Rush: "I have no other objections to your dream, but that it is not history. It may be prophecy." Indeed, it was. Silence persisted for a few more years, and the eerier part of Rush's "dream," which Adams did not address, required some more years to become "history." Yet it did, too. For Rush also predicted in 1809 that the two patriarchs "sunk into the grave nearly at the same time," which in fact they would, on the day of America's national jubilee, the fiftieth anniversary of Independence. How could Benjamin Rush have known that![42]

John Adams took the initiative as Rush's dream had stipulated. On January 1, 1812, he took the liberty of dispatching a copy of the just-published *Lectures on Rhetoric and Oratory*, authored by John Quincy Adams, then professor of rhetoric at Harvard. "I wish you Sir many happy New Years," Adams bade Jefferson.

Jefferson prepared a long and thoughtful reply. "A letter from you calls up recollections very dear to my mind," he wrote tenderly on January 21. "It carries me back to the times when, beset with difficulties and dangers, we were fellow laborers in the same cause, struggling for what is most valuable to man, his right of self-government."[43] The language of the heart was always Jefferson's first recourse, finding emotional expression for what to him was the idea of America.

Adams and he had that in common—both having been present at the creation, and both instrumental in pressing for nationhood. For Jefferson, their struggle in 1776 had been like an ocean passage, agitated and uncertain: "Laboring always at the same oar, with some wave ever ahead threatening to overwhelm us and yet passing harmlessly under our bark, we knew not how, we rode through the storm with heart and hand, and made a happy port."

The metaphor of the sea was a literary device that Jefferson employed frequently over his years as a letter writer. In writing his grandson just a few years earlier, he had bewailed public conflict, referring to "the boisterous ocean of political passions." In Jefferson's day, the sea voyage was a microcosm of the journey of life, just as one can come to a crossroads, experience a bumpy road, or reach a dead end figuratively as well as literally. In his "My Head and My Heart" letter to Maria Cosway in 1786, the head observed: "The art of life is the art of avoiding pain: and he is the best pilot who steers clearest of the rocks and shoals with which it is beset." To his Philadelphia landlady, Jefferson wrote a short while later, "Laid up in port, for life, as I thought myself at one time, I am thrown out to sea, and an unknown one to me. By so slender a thread do all our plans of life hang!" And to lawyer St. George Tucker, in 1793: "What an ocean is life! And how our barks get separated in beating through it." In the larger sense, then, the sea reflected both inner turmoil and untamed nature for eighteenth-century Americans.

But in writing Adams in 1812, Jefferson employed the sea metaphor to reflect on a successful passage. They had made this voyage together, moreover "with heart and hand," and arrived at their retired state happily. As he moved past the first two pages of his letter, touching on recent news from Europe, Jefferson next chastised himself: "But whither is senile garrulity leading me? Into politics, of which I have taken final leave.... I have given up newspapers in exchange for Tacitus and Thucydides, for Newton and Euclid; and I find myself much the happier."

While this may not have been precisely true—Jefferson could not entirely neglect affairs of state, as Presidents Madison and Monroe continued to call on him for advice—he intended to give a sign to Adams that his partisan spirit would not interfere with the restoration of their friendship. He wanted to minimize discussion of any subject that might threaten to disrupt harmony, and he had in fact returned to reading classical authors, in the original Latin and Greek, for pure enjoyment. Now he would have someone of equal erudition with whom to converse about the ancients.

Before winding up this first letter, Jefferson could not resist a reference to the seminal moment in their lives: July 4, 1776. "Of the signers of the Declaration of Independence I see now living not more than a half dozen on your side of the Potomack, and, on this side, myself alone. You and I have been wonderfully spared."

From here, Jefferson manipulated his theme—the process of aging—so as to establish his high regard for Adams. He did so, drawing upon eighteenth-century epistolary convention, by engaging in literary wit, by expressing anticipation of learning about all that Adams might have to say about himself, and by modestly asserting that his correspondent was greater and worthier of honors than he.

Jefferson was nearing his sixty-ninth birthday, and Adams was past seventy-six. Turning to wit in his composition, the writer now remarked that he lived "in the midst of my grandchildren" and had been recently "promoted" to great-grandfather. Then, apologizing for a long, self-indulgent letter "full of egotisms," the Virginian, who could ride horseback but had trouble walking, insisted that he would rather hear about Adams's health ("your habits, occupations and enjoyments"). In doing so, he hoped to have "the pleasure of knowing that, in the race of life, you do not keep, in it's physical decline, the same distance ahead of me which you have done in political honors and atchievements." With this self-deprecatory reference—claiming that Adams outdistanced him in political legacy—and linking this to his hope that Adams suffered from the aging process less than he, despite his extra years—Jefferson was trying to display a generous spirit. It was a good first letter from an acknowledged political adversary, and he signed off: "No circumstances have lessened the interest I feel in these particulars respecting yourself; none have suspended for one moment my sincere esteem for you; and I now salute you with unchanged affections and respect."

On February 3, Adams was astonished to receive a letter from Jefferson dated January 23. Given a horse-drawn postal service, and "Roads so embarrassed," as Adams described American traveling conditions, eight days from Central Virginia to the neighborhood of Boston was almost beyond belief. The postmark read "Milton," a town just three miles from Adams's Quincy home, and he first wondered why it would take eight whole days for a letter to travel three miles. Then he thought he recognized the handwriting on the envelope and finally discovered that there was also a town of Milton just down the hill from Jefferson's Monticello. He immediately wrote Jefferson back, delighted "that the Communication between Us is much easier, surer and may be more frequent than I had ever believed or suspected to be possible."

As to Jefferson's professed abandonment of the newspapers, Adams answered, "What an Exchange have you made? Of Newspapers for Newton! Rising from the lower deep of the lowest deep of Dulness and Bathos to the Contemplation of the Heavens and the heavens of Heavens." Adams was a livelier wit than Jefferson was, less cautious if less crisp. Adams was spontaneous, generally saying whatever came to his mind; Jefferson hesitated, pondered, and calculated until he found a choice phrase, always aiming before he struck. This was the difference between them—and not just in letter-writing style.

Regarding matters of health and aging, Adams reported: "I walk every fair day, sometimes 3 or 4 miles. Ride now and then but very rarely more than ten or fifteen Miles. But I have a Complaint that Nothing but the Ground can cure, that is the Palsy; a kind of Paralytic Affection of the Nerves, which makes my hands tremble, and renders it difficult to write at all and impossible to write well." As much as medical complaints would find their way into most of their letters, nothing would curb their extraordinary conversation now that it had started again.

They touched on politics—Adams especially—as the War of 1812 approached. "Whether you or I were right," Adams alluded to their respective administrations, "Posterity must judge."[44] But they did much better and carried on with more enthusiasm and less restriction when the subject was science and historic literature. In the first year after the resumption of their friendship, Adams wrote eight times, Jefferson five.

Then, Benjamin Rush died. "Another of our friends of 76. is gone, my dear Sir," Jefferson began his letter of May 27, 1813, "another of the Cosigners of the independance of our country. And a better man, than Rush, could not have left us, more benevolent, more learned, of finer genius, or more honest. We too must go; and that ere long." It was far from the last time that Jefferson and Adams would ruminate, in print, about death.

Letters could not stop for death. As we have seen, letters so often bore news of someone's passing that they had to be augmented with other, less doleful topics. So after commenting on Rush's moral excellence, Jefferson moved right into a discussion about books, in this case about the credibility of historical research and the state of knowledge about human origins. Musing about whether the

American Indian was related to the Persians, he reflected on the commonality among languages: "All languages may be called the same, as being made up of the same primitive sounds, expressed by the letters of the different alphabets." After a meandering look at classifications of various languages, he concluded that any search for a clear understanding would be fruitless in their lifetimes: "The question of Indian origins, like many others pushed to a certain height, must recieve the same answer, 'Ignoro.'"[45]

This sort of "thinking on paper" represented what letter writing meant to Cicero, the well-published virtuoso of ancient Rome: uncensored thought, or moral-philosophical exposition, dressed in the garb of friendly correspondence. Both Jefferson and Adams believed, as Cicero did, that epistolary friendship carried self-cultivation to new heights and that letters ultimately illuminated the world. If there was such a thing as "virtuous passion"—and the eighteenth century conceived that there was—this was the classical consciousness that Jefferson and Adams sought to preserve by writing.

As Adams continued provocatively to dredge up the political past, Jefferson waded in. On June 15, 1813, prompted by Adams's reference to a new book on the Unitarians, the freethinking Virginian displayed his enduring bitterness toward New England's clerical opposition, whose alarm over his supposed rejection of religion was derived from his stated position in support of the separation of church and state. The new publication contained Jefferson's private letter to Dr. Joseph Priestley of March 21, 1801 (see above). Jefferson had forgotten all about it. Adams repeated back to Jefferson his combustible phrase of a dozen years before: "What an effort, my dear Sir, [Jefferson had written Priestley] of bigotry in Politics & Religion have we gone through! The barbarians really flattered themselves they should be able to bring back the time of Vandalism, when ignorance put every thing into the hands of power & priestcraft." The revelation of this letter would, Jefferson predicted, "gratify the priesthood"—his preferred term for certain arrogant clergymen of Adams's part of the country. "They wish it to be believed that he can have no religion who advocates it's freedom."

To Jefferson, letters of this kind—shared confidences—were meant to be treasured as ardent utterances directed only to the intended recipient. They were, as Cicero had said of his own familiar letters, solicitous, anxious affections, sincere expressions of the inner life. Jefferson told Adams that the politically explosive letter to Priestley was personal, and "never meant to trouble the public mind. Whether the character of the times is justly portrayed or not, posterity will decide." With that phrase, "posterity will decide," Jefferson repeated to Adams precisely what Adams had written to him the year before concerning the justness of his and Jefferson's presidential decisions.

"You have right and reason to feel and to resent the breach of Confidence," Adams commiserated on June 25. "I have had enough of the same kind of Treachery and Perfidy practiced upon me, to know how to sympathize with you." He agreed wholeheartedly with Jefferson that the publication of private letters was a form of "Tyranny" and such infringements on privacy only served to "suppress the free communication of Soul to Soul."

Jefferson's next, written on June 27 (before he had read what would be a welcome letter from Adams), showed him returned to a pacified temperament. In consideration of human nature and history, and expecting no better than what political disputes were bound to bring, he observed: "Men have differed in opinion, and been divided into parties by these opinions, from the first origin of societies; and in all governments where they have been permitted freely to think and speak. The same political parties which now agitate the U.S. have existed thro' all time."

He wished only to ensure that Adams would not allow their former political differences to distance them again. In this he was at his most sincere. "The renewal of these old discussions, my friend, would be equally useless and irksome," Jefferson entreated. "To the volumes then written on these subjects, human ingenuity can add nothing new." It seems to have relieved Jefferson to say this.

He went on, not quite as convincingly. "My mind has been long fixed to bow to the judgment of the world, who will judge me by my acts, and will never take counsel from me as to what that judgment shall be." To believe otherwise would be arrogance. Jefferson knew that, yet he was human. He hoped that his political administration would be hailed by posterity; his correspondence with his faithful political allies makes this plain.

Protestations to the contrary, Jefferson wanted to influence how history regarded him. He understood that what he was saying to Adams was true: he could not dictate to future biographers. Though Jefferson was a supremely well-organized letter writer, a plantation owner accustomed to command, and such a planner that he eventually wrote his own epitaph, he could not shape his own political legacy, not even in his own time. Echoes of the more strident and inflexible of Adams's Federalist party continued to cloud his retirement; they were producing their own books of recent political history and their marked antipathy toward Jefferson made him inflexible, too. No matter how genial he was in his late years' communications with Adams, he did not adopt a confessional posture. He carefully crafted the persona we read and perceive, and he did not waver or doubt himself. He remained keenly aware of the future political value of his letters because he knew we would be reading them.

There were some issues that no length of correspondence would ever be able to resolve. On the touchy subject of religion, though, Jefferson did the best he could. On August 22, 1813, he offered his friend a quintessentially Jeffersonian perspective: "I very much suspect that if thinking men would have the courage to think for themselves, and to speak what they think, it would be found they do not differ in religious opinions, as much as is supposed." On September 14, Adams put a coda on the discussion in his own inimitable style: "It has been long, very long a settled opinion in my Mind that there is now, never will be, and never was but one being who can Understand the Universe. And that it is not only vain but wicked for insects to pretend to comprehend it."

The friendship thrived as these two intellectually nimble correspondents discussed conscience, reason, and revelation with extended references to philosophers and theologians, to Plato and the Eclectics, to the Testaments and the Talmud. They agreed to disagree about the political direction of America. In what appears the longest of all his retirement letters, Jefferson wrote Adams on October 28, 1813, why he regarded his country as special:

Before the establishment of the American states, nothing was known to
History but the Man of the old world, crouded within limits either small

or overcharged, and steeped in the vices which that situation generates. A government adapted to such men would be one thing; but a very different one that for the Man of these states. Here every one may have land to labor for himself if he chuses.... And such men may safely and advantageously reserve to themselves a wholesome controul over their public affairs, and a degree of freedom, which in the hands of the Canaille of the cities of Europe, would be instantly perverted to the demolition of every thing public and private.

His critique of Europe went back decades. He regarded the Old World of his lifetime as an exhausted place in the process of degeneration, its very atmosphere unhealthy. America, to him, was fruitful and prolific, conducive to the growth of generous feeling, thus requiring the support of a government that prized individual liberty.

Jefferson's singular hope for the Old World, he proceeded to tell Adams, was at once moral and intellectual: "Science has liberated the ideas of those who read and reflect, and the American example has kindled feelings of right in the people." If aristocracy were to "finally shrink into insignificance," then Europe might be saved, just as he believed America had been saved by Jeffersonian democracy: "It suffices for us, if the moral and physical condition of our own citizens qualifies them to select the able and good for the direction of their government, with a recurrence of elections at such short periods as will enable them to displace an unfaithful servant before the mischief he meditates may be irremediable." The principles of representative democracy had sustained Thomas Jefferson's optimism.

"I have thus stated my opinion," he drew to a close, "on a point on which we differ, not with a view to controversy, for we are both too old to change opinions which are the result of a long life of inquiry and reflection; but on the suggestion of a former letter of yours, that we ought not to die before we have explained ourselves to each other." One can sense the letter writer's catharsis as he put down his pen.

In a sense, Jefferson's vaunted belief in the sturdiness of reason was realized in his exchanges with old John Adams. Jefferson's ideal, as expressed in his first inaugural address, was a polity in which differences of opinion did not have to produce permanent division; there could be disagreement without dislike. Adams's distrust of the democratic impulse and Jefferson's implicit faith in ordinary people did not have to result in a renewal of their rupture; for after a lifetime of inviting controversy, these two self-assured political intellects were better friends than ever. As lovers of an honest quest for knowledge, equally devoted to the pursuit of happiness for the society they cherished, they had come to understand human difference without impugning their adversary's motives.

As Jefferson passed seventy, he was prone to writing more about physical debility. On July 5, 1814, his metaphor for the body as a failing mechanism was a timepiece ticking down its final hours: "our machines have now been running for 70. or 80. years, and we must expect that, worn as they are, here a pivot, there a wheel, now a pinion, next a spring, will be giving way: and however we may tinker them up for awhile, all will at length surcease motion." Adams's prompt reply: "I am sometimes afraid that my 'Machine' will not 'surcease motion' soon enough."

On March 2, 1816, Adams posed a "frivolous" question, as he himself termed it: "Would you go back to your Cradle and live over again your 70 Years?" Confirming that "it is a good world on the whole," Jefferson recurred to a sea metaphor in making his affirmative reply: "I steer my bark with Hope in the head, leaving Fear astern. My hopes indeed sometimes fail; but not oftener than the forebodings of the gloomy." This time, Jefferson's sea was not unduly boisterous. And Adams, enjoying the exchange, came back: "I admire your Navigation and should like to sail with you."

On August 1, 1816, still conversing about the value of life amid the unavoidable infirmities of age and the grief associated with loss, Jefferson appraised: "There is a ripeness of time for death, regarding others as well as ourselves, when it is reasonable we should drop off, and make room for another growth. When we have lived our generation out, we should not wish to encroach on another. I enjoy good health; I am happy in what is around me. Yet I assure you I am ripe for leaving all, this year, this day, this hour." More than he feared bodily decay, he said, he feared another affliction that a number of the aged suffered: "body without mind." Finishing his thought with elegance, the imaginative Jefferson signed off, "I like the dreams of the future better than the history of the past. So good night. I will dream on, always fancying that Mrs Adams and yourself are by my side marking the progress and the obliquities of ages and countries."

Unbeknownst to them, they had ten intellectually vigorous years yet allotted to them. It was not long, however, before Jefferson returned to the subject of grief: he could not accept that nature had provided the emotion of grief for any useful purpose. Supplying many brilliant examples, Adams rationalized that "sad men ... tossed and buffeted in the Vicissitudes of Life" were best equipped to teach humanity. However, Jefferson maintained in his letter of October 14, 1816: "Those afflictions cloud too great a portion of life to find a counterpoise in any benefits derived from it's uses." The only value of grief that he could fathom was in preparing people for their own deaths; the "salutary effects of grief ... prepares us to lose ourselves also without repugnance."

They went on discussing politics, Greek, language, sensation, and meaning. In their last years, Jefferson's optimism remained constant. Referring to the accomplishments of their generation, even as the controversy between North and South grew, he wrote on September 12, 1820: "I will not believe our labors are lost. I shall not die without a hope that light and liberty are on a steady advance.... In short, the flames kindled on the 4th. of July 1776. have spread over too much of the globe to be extinguished by the feeble engines of despotism. On the contrary they will consume those engines, and all who work for them."

Yet death was a preoccupation, and the right wrist Jefferson had dislocated in Paris in 1786 stiffened, making writing painful. On June 1, 1822, Jefferson penned: "When the friends of our youth are all gone, and a generation is risen around us whom we know not, is death an evil?" Recall his last letter to Maria Cosway, in 1820, in which he similarly posed: "For after one's friends are all gone before them, and our faculties leaving us too, one by one, why wish to linger in mere vegetation, as a solitary trunk in a desolate field, from which all it's former companions have disappeared." Adams, at eighty-six, assured his Virginia friend that death was not an evil: "It is a blessing to the individual, and to the world. Yet we ought not to wish for it till life becomes insupportable; we must wait the pleasure and convenience of this great teacher."

It would seem that Jefferson came round to Adams's calm. After more conversations passed between them regarding God and truth, he analogized heaven to a reunion of the political class of '76, signing off his letter of April 11, 1823, just two days before his eightieth birthday: "I join you cordially, and await [God's] time and will with more readiness than reluctance. May we meet there again, in Congress, with our antient Colleagues, and recieve them with the seal of approbation 'Well done, good and faithful servants.'"

Once more, on December 18, 1825, Thomas Jefferson reminded John Adams, who had now reached his ninetieth year, that he loved life enough, despite its attendant griefs, to live it over again: "My spirits have never failed me except under those paroxysms of grief which you, as well as myself, have experienced in every form: and with good health and good spirits the pleasures surely outweigh the pains of life. Why not then taste them again, fat and lean together."

These two mighty intellects, men of passion and purpose, had ruminated across time and space on the subject of mortality, and in the end had the spectacular (many columnists and eulogists said miraculous) distinction of dying alike on the fiftieth Fourth of July. As politicians and presidents, they ruled in times of turbulence. As letter writers, they ruled over a medium of peace.

View from Cabinet to Jefferson's Bedroom. (Robert C. Lautman/Thomas Jefferson Foundation, Inc.)

Chapter Eleven

DEATHBED ADIEU

Jefferson appreciated poetry, as he appreciated literature and history generally. Though he loved to play with language, he was not known as a man with a poet's compulsion. In 1782, he and his dying wife had jointly written down lines from Laurence Sterne on a square piece of paper, which he kept for the balance of his long life. In 1826, as he himself was confined to his room and conscious of his emotional debt to the living, Jefferson composed lines of verse for his one surviving daughter, Martha Randolph. In this final poem, he referred to her sister and mother, whom he called "Two Seraphs." He also used the metaphor of life as a voyage to chart his having crossed the ocean and arrived at a trouble-free shore. Jefferson titled the poem "A death-bed Adieu. Th:J to MR."

Life's visions are vanished, it's dreams are no more.
Dear friends of the bosom, why bathed in tears?
I go to my fathers; I welcome the shore,
which crowns all my hopes, or which buries my cares.
Then farewell my dear, my lov'd daughter, Adieu!
The last pang in life is in parting from you!
Two Seraphs await me, long shrouded in death:
I will bear them your love on my last parting breath.[46]

Jefferson's paperweights, seal, inkwell, quill, and fountain pen. (Edward Owen/Thomas Jefferson Foundation, Inc.)

Chapter Twelve

CONCLUSION

A mind always employed is always happy. This is the true secret, the grand recipe for felicity. The idle are the only wretched. In a world which furnishes so many emploiments which are useful, and so many which are amusing, it is our own fault if we ever know what ennui is.[47]

"Perhaps nothing so inspires good writing as travel to new places." When he wrote these words to his then sixteen-year-old daughter Martha, on May 21, 1787, Thomas Jefferson was traveling on a barge along the Canal de Languedoc, in southern France. He employed the medium of the familiar letter in many ways: as a tool to impart wisdom, a diversion by which he could speculate freely, an experimental mode for testing out ideas with trusted associates, or simply to promote what was then called fellow feeling, and what we now term friendship.

Looking at the turning point in his life, the American Revolution, we can glean something of Jefferson's sense of what that moment of political change meant for him by his later writings. In "My Head and My Heart," the head calculated and compared and found Great Britain's "wealth and numbers" clearly superior to the colonies. Yet America's heart supplied "enthusiasm" against those "wealth and numbers," and in doing so, "we saved our country." Jefferson liked to think that the investment of heart always led in the right direction.

He spent his life reaching out to others. Like everyone else in the eighteenth century, he was obliged to struggle against logistical difficulties associated with communications, and he strove toward a more open expression of sentiments when convention dictated politeness over any truer self-revelation. In mastering the medium, he wavered between artificial forms of communication and the desire for a more sincere disclosure of his own inner voice.

Letter writing established social authority in Jefferson's world, much more so than writing of any kind determines power in the technological age. Reputations rose and fell according to the production of pamphlets, newspaper essays, and public speeches. Letters were published, generally with the letter writer's full knowledge, so as to sustain public conversations concerning matters of national import. Similarly, ideas gleaned from the study of past models (such as Cicero's letters and speeches or the letters and treatises by English thinkers of the seventeenth and early eighteenth centuries) helped revolutionary Americans establish a dignified bearing, as they instituted a "republic of letters" among themselves. Through these letters, they began to view their new nation as a legitimate moral force in the world.

When in retirement Jefferson wrote Adams about politics and religion, he was continuing to promote the "republic of letters." He knew the correspondence would eventually become part of a canon of American literary expression and thus was conscious of writing for posterity. Yet he disclosed feelings that are unceremoniously private. He maintained a traditional view of letters as texts possessing both a private and a public character; letters served as an emotional release, yet they were meant to be preserved and eventually copied. The burden on the letter writer, in this case, was reflected in the certain knowledge of the larger historic value of his thoughts.

So, finally, how do we "read" Jefferson? Perhaps the best, most realistic way is to view him as a product of an era, and so we should have no expectations of him that were not readily possible then. He was a well-born man with a desire for social advancement, thus fairly typical of his time and place; but he was also an unusually avid book collector and lover of knowledge with an extraordinary talent for transmitting affections—"affections" is the key here, a word he used extensively, in both public addresses and in letters less certainly intended for the public. He understood "affections" as a benevolent temperament that produced personal advantage and administrative achievement. How did he come to such a formulation? By reading the discourses of others who had sought truth in experiments of the mind. He became a master of eloquence by consulting earlier masters of eloquence. His literary breeding, unlike his legal training, was largely self-taught.

He understood the language of friendship and saw the opportunity to apply it to republican politics. This achievement required an inquisitive mind, an amiability that was not forced, and a rare literary consciousness.

Jefferson was not necessarily the most original writer of his generation, but he certainly expanded the range of words in a most intriguing way so that what he wrote two centuries ago resonates still. In the same sense that we can appreciate a Shakespearean play that captures human emotions which time has not altered, we can read Jefferson and know that he continues to speak to American purposes.

We of the twenty-first century still have something in common with Thomas Jefferson: we value freedom of conscience, insisting that the life of the mind must not be compromised.

Notes

1 TJ to Anne Randolph Bankhead, May 26, 1811, *The Family Letters of Thomas Jefferson*, ed. Edwin Morris Betts and James Adam Bear, Jr. (Charlottesville: University Press of Virginia, 1986; reprint, Columbia, Mo.: 1966), 400. Hereafter cited as *Family Letters*.

2 John Catanzariti, "Thomas Jefferson: Correspondent," *Proceedings of the Massachusetts Historical Society* 102 (Boston, 1990): 1–20.

3 TJ to James Madison, Jan. 30, 1787, *The Papers of Thomas Jefferson*, ed. Julian P. Boyd, et al. (Princeton: Princeton University Press, 1950–), 11:97. Hereafter cited as *Papers*.

4 TJ to George Logan, June 20, 1816, *The Writings of Thomas Jefferson*, ed. Paul Leicester Ford. 10 vols. (New York: G. P. Putnam's Sons, 1904–05), 10:27.

5 Among the many distinctive interpretive works on Jefferson's Declaration, see especially Carl Becker, *The Declaration of Independence* (New York, 1922), which still stands out after more than three-quarters of a century; Jay Fliegelman, *Declaring Independence: Jefferson, Natural Language, and the Culture of Performance* (Stanford: Stanford University Press, 1993); and Pauline Meier, *American Scripture* (New York: Knopf, 1997). The various drafts, and final version of the Declaration, are detailed in *Papers*, vol. 1.

6 *Orations Delivered at the Request of the Inhabitants of the Town of Boston to Commemorate the Evening of the Fifth of March, 1770* (Boston, 1785), 7–16.

7 Lines copied from *Tristram Shandy* by Martha and Thomas Jefferson before her death on September 6, 1782. *Papers*, 6:196.

8 *Jefferson's Literary Commonplace Book*, ed. Douglas L. Wilson (Princeton: Princeton University Press, 1989), 62, 182–83. I treat Sterne's fiction at greater length in *The Inner Jefferson: Portrait of a Grieving Optimist* (Charlottesville: University of Virginia Press, 1995), chap. 2: "Jefferson and Sterne."

9 TJ to Peter Carr, Aug. 10, 1787, *Papers*, 12:15.

10 *Jefferson's Memorandum Books*, ed. James A. Bear, Jr. and Lucia C. Stanton. 2 vols. (Princeton: Princeton University Press, 1997), 1:521.

11 The very faint original is at the James Monroe Museum, Fredericksburg, Virginia.

12 TJ to Maria Cosway, Oct. 12, 1786, *Papers*, 10:443–453.

13 G.K. Van Hogendorp Papers, cited in *Papers*, 7:82n.

14 TJ to William S. Smith, Oct. 22, 1786, *Papers*, 10:478.

[15] Jefferson's famous dialogue has been reprinted in several collections, including the *Papers* as cited above in note twelve, as well as *Jefferson Abroad*, ed. Douglas L. Wilson and Lucia Stanton (New York: Modern Library, 1999), 96–106; and *The Portable Thomas Jefferson*, ed. Merrill D. Peterson (New York: Penguin Books, 1975), 400–412.

[16] The letters of November and December 1786 are in the Manuscripts Division, Alderman Library, University of Virginia.

[17] TJ to Maria Cosway, Dec. 27, 1820, in Helen Duprey Bullock, *My Head and My Heart* (New York: G.P. Putnam's Sons, 1945), 176–77.

[18] TJ to Martha Jefferson Randolph, Mar. 24, 1793, *Family Letters*, 114.

[19] TJ to Martha Jefferson Randolph, Jan. 26, 1793, *Family Letters*, 110.

[20] TJ to Martha Jefferson Randolph, May 8, 1791, *Family Letters*, 80.

[21] TJ to Martha Jefferson Randolph, Aug. 14, 1791, *Family Letters*, 89.

[22] TJ to Martha Jefferson Randolph, May 31, 1798 and Jan. 23, 1799, *Family Letters*, 164, 172.

[23] TJ to Martha Jefferson Randolph, Jan. 1, 1799, *Family Letters*, 170–71.

[24] TJ to Martha Jefferson Randolph, Feb. 7, 1799, *Family Letters*, 173–74.

[25] TJ to Elbridge Gerry, Jan. 26, 1799, *The Writings of Thomas Jefferson*, ed. Paul Leicester Ford, 7:325–35.

[26] Jefferson's first inaugural address is reprinted in several sources, including *The Portable Jefferson*, ed. Peterson, 290–95.

[27] Benjamin Rush to TJ, Mar. 12, 1801, *Letters of Benjamin Rush*, ed. L. H. Butterfield, 2 vols. ([Philadelphia] : American Philosophical Society, 1951), 2:831–33.

[28] The political character of sensibility is the subject of my book *Sentimental Democracy: The Evolution of America's Romantic Self-Image* (New York: Hill and Wang, 1999).

[29] TJ to Joseph Priestley, Mar. 21, 1801, in *The Portable Thomas Jefferson*, ed. Peterson, 483–85. Jefferson's relationship with Priestley, along with Priestley's political correspondence, is detailed in Jenny Graham, *Revolutionary in Exile: The Emigration of Joseph Priestley to America, 1794–1804* (Philadelphia: American Philosophical Society, 1995).

[30] TJ to John Page, June 25, 1804, Thomas Jefferson Papers, Library of Congress.

[31] TJ to John Page, Feb. 21, 1770, *Papers*, 1:34–36.

[32] TJ to John Page, July 15, 1763, *Papers*, 1:10–11.

33 TJ to John Page, January 23, 1764, *Papers*, 1:15.

34 John Page to TJ, Apr. 6, 1776, *Papers*, 1:287.

35 John Page to TJ, June 2, 1779; TJ to Page, June 3, 1779, *Papers*, 2:278–79.

36 TJ to James Madison, Dec. 8, 1784, *Papers*, 7:558.

37 John Page to TJ, Sept. 13, 1808, Thomas Jefferson Papers, Library of Congress.

38 TJ to Thomas Jefferson Randolph, Nov. 24, 1808, *Family Letters*, 364.

39 TJ to Thomas Jefferson Randolph, Oct. 24, 1808, *Family Letters*, 353.

40 The substance of Jefferson's rules for contending with the world, which follow, are from TJ to Thomas Jefferson Randolph, Nov. 24, 1808, *Family Letters*, 362–65.

41 TJ to John Adams, Aug. 1, 1816, *The Adams-Jefferson Letters: The Complete Correspondence Between Thomas Jefferson and Abigail and John Adams*, ed. Lester J. Cappon (Chapel Hill: University of North Carolina Press, 1959), 484. Hereafter cited as *Adams-Jefferson Letters*.

42 Benjamin Rush to John Adams, Oct. 17, 1809, *Letters of Benjamin Rush*, ed. Butterfield, 2:1021–22.

43 John Adams to TJ, Jan. 1, 1812; TJ to Adams, Jan. 21, 1812, *Adams-Jefferson Letters*, 290–92. Subsequent dated references are drawn from the same volume.

44 Adams to TJ, May 1, 1812, *Adams-Jefferson Letters*, 301.

45 TJ to Adams, May 27, 1813, *Adams-Jefferson Letters*, 323–24.

46 Sarah N. Randolph, *The Domestic Life of Thomas Jefferson* (Charlottesville: Thomas Jefferson Memorial Foundation, 1967; reprint, 1871), 429.

47 TJ to Martha Jefferson, May 21, 1787, *Papers*, 11:370.

Suggested Reading

Of the innumerable works that deal with the life of Thomas Jefferson, few examine his literary interests and letter-writing habits. More than a half-century has gone by since the original publication of Karl Lehmann's *Thomas Jefferson, American Humanist*, republished by the University Press of Virginia in 1985. This delightful book examines Jefferson's classical consciousness and love of learning, basic ingredients in his attraction to the written word. My own *The Inner Jefferson: Portrait of a Grieving Optimist* (University Press of Virginia, 1995) concentrates on the value of reading and writing during Jefferson's formative years. It also establishes the influences on his sentimental style, relates his private life—as revealed in letters—to his public pronouncements, and charts his struggle to assert a personal vision for America over the course of a long political career.

Douglas L. Wilson has made several notable contributions to the study of Jefferson's writing, most remarkably in the reconstruction of *Jefferson's Literary Commonplace Book*, part of the *Papers of Thomas Jefferson*, Second Series (Princeton University Press, 1989). This volume discloses changes in Jefferson's handwriting over time so as to determine the order in which he extracted and recorded favorite passages from poetry and literature. Professor Wilson also contributed an excellent essay, "Jefferson and the Republic of Letters" to Peter S. Onuf, ed., *Jeffersonian Legacies* (University Press of Virginia, 1994). Another essay in that volume, offering a valuable glimpse of Jefferson's domestic life and his association of familial notions with a broader political vision, is Jan Lewis's "'The Blessings of Domestic Society:' Thomas Jefferson's Family and the Transformation of American Politics."

There are many ways to gain access to Jefferson's letters. The most complete modern collection, available in many libraries, is the *Papers of Thomas Jefferson* (Princeton University Press, 1950–). These contain virtually every document extant that pertain to Jefferson's writing life, from his seventeenth year. Because of the comprehensive nature of this project, the *Papers* as of this date are nearing their thirtieth volume and have yet to reach Jefferson's presidency. However, the concurrent publication of Jefferson's *Retirement Papers* is now underway at Monticello and promises to be a rich resource for anyone interested in the evocative writings of Jefferson's post-presidential years.

More compact collections of Jefferson's writings include: *The Portable Thomas Jefferson*, edited by Merrill D. Peterson (Viking Penguin, 1975); *The Adams-Jefferson Letters: The Complete Correspondence between Thomas Jefferson and Abigail and John Adams* (University of North Carolina Press, 1959; reissued 1987); *The Republic of Letters: The Correspondence between Thomas Jefferson and James Madison, 1776–1826*, edited by James Morton Smith (W.W. Norton, 1995); *The Family Letters of Thomas Jefferson*, edited by Edwin Morris Betts and James Adam Bear, Jr. (University of Missouri Press, 1966; reissued by the University Press of Virginia in 1986); and *Jefferson Abroad*, edited by Douglas L. Wilson and Lucia Stanton (Modern Library, 1999).

—ANDREW BURSTEIN

INDEX